The Path to Awakening

CASTLES
OF
POVERTY

by

_jema_sid

Publised by Ibukku, LLC
www.ibukku.com
Graphic Design: Índigo Estudio Gráfico
Copyright © 2022 Jesús Edgar Medina Adame
ISBN Paperback: 978-1-68574-228-7
ISBN eBook: 978-1-68574-229-4
LCCN: 2022918194

Table of Content

Behind My Eyes

My ignorance reaches
what my wisdom
cannot imagine.

_jema_sid

Fragments of the Prologue

L a Rosa is to meditate on our concerns, it is not to criticize kings or pawns, the poor or the rich. At the same time, it is a reminder of what we could do to get to know ourselves better first.

It is a dramatic love story that shows us that we can dream as far as infinity without straying from those who need our actions of goodness on the earth that nourishes our bodies with its fruit branches.

The smallest proves that it can become the greatest when comes out of conformity that this reality has formed.

Dedicated to my mother:

Emma Adame Almaraz

Chapter 1
A Rainbow in the Dark

"There was not much to eat except how little you could save from the trash. People throw more than they need to live," said Philip.

Philip told me what was lifelike in the garbage dump and how he managed to get clean food every day for his family. It was a daily feat to get just a piece of bread or even something to drink because there were not many facilities to get what anyone needs to have a dignified, clean and healthy life. On the contrary, they were the forgotten of the world and its indifference, of the lack of charity of these broken hearts by greed and selfishness.

These are the ones who approve corruption by interests of goods or services, forgetting those who just need a little mercy. Being only that which the innocents expect from them because they got tired of waiting for the broken promises of these greedy ones, who are indifferent to the innocents who die when the powerful forces of social show masters collide. Somehow, who could judge them by their ignorance, to these puppets of evil who are carried away by the pleasures they obtain in life, in exchange for slavery in serving the purpose of their evil master. And perhaps, we are the ones who make a mistake in judging them and we live in the opinion of our own perception of reality, and trying to change them, we waste the moments on vane things alien to ourselves, disregarding the purpose, which is revealed when rediscovering oneself.

At the garbage dump, the daily competition Philip had to deal with was unfair and immoral, and it did not seem like the bullies would ever leave power. These criminals always seized any object that seems to have some value, for this reason, they did not let the people from the community benefit from any means that would help them get out of the hole in which they were held.

"They entertain us, they keep us distracted so we don't fly," Philip said, referring to those enlightened by greed and power.

Since he was a child, Philip remembers fighting with other children who snatched the little he found out of his hands. Sometimes he was beaten for claiming his find, or for defending others from the greed of these dishonest abusive wretches, lacking in honesty and respect for others. On many of those occasions, he ended up crying lying next to the pile of garbage, while the others bragged about what had been taken from him by mocking his miserable person and his wretched fate.

Those who are poor know that even among them there are some who are poorer, whom we marginalize labeling them as the miserable, whom even the beggars despise. Philip's family was one of the most miserable in the community, and like many more families, they suffered from discrimination and injustice by those who always seized everything that others found. Those abusers controlled all the collections that people made from the piles of garbage and charged a fee to the collectors to collect the garbage that came from the city, from a rich neighborhood, or from middle-class people. Whoever did not pay the fee imposed by the executioners, did not have the right to collect the piles of the best garbage.

There were ranks inherited from generation to generation among the complex community that had formed in that wretched place away from the hand of God. Philip's family was the lowest ranking in all generations up to him; for they never had the privilege that other families had to collect among the garbage that came from those communities with better resources. Of course, community leaders were always the ones who got the best out of everything because even though someone found something of value in their turn to collect, as they had to go through a kind of inspection point by those abusers, the objects that the leader considered of his interest were seized. No one could even say a single word to complain, for fear they would suffer retaliation by their executioners. Those who paid the highest share had the opportunity to collect among the best-rate garbage, while those who did not have much to give, were content to collect among the garbage that others had already collected; that is, among the leftovers of the garbage that other collectors threw away; among the garbage from the garbage.

There were days when Philip only ate the waste left over from the day before, and not even crumbs at times. He did not have any money because he could not find something useful to sell, well it was of no importance to him to sell what was invaluable in his heart, such as the things his father had inherited for him and his mother's memories.

The executioner of the community degraded him in such a way and mercilessly, giving him no chance in absolutely nothing, making his life even more miserable. There was resentment against him and his family to a wretched degree, well wherever they found him, he was physically and emotionally abused by them; besides, they would not let anyone help him in anything, or else they would receive retaliation with which he always threatened them.

On one of those occasions when hunger caused him to lose his fear, he ventured to a pile of garbage restricted by the community leader on which he did not have any permit to recollect. But he dared to approach because hunger pushed him to see if he could find anything he could eat. On that occasion, by the way, a lady let out crying when she saw him eat something that he had found thrown among the waste. Well, the moment Philip found the piece of bread, he immediately put it in his mouth so that no one could take it off, and as a wild animal defended his piece of thing, with a dog famine. At that moment, the man in charge of watching the heap of more categories saw him and kicked him out of the place, leaving him without air but without dropping his piece of French bread that he had found, which was already almost as hard as a brick. The kick helped him, for in that instant he was drowning and as the air was removed from his lungs, unclogged the piece of French stone stuck in his throat. What a disappointment the result, regarding the intention that man had against Philip, who instead of harming him, ended up saving his life. As he could he stood up after taking some air and walked away very happy with his piece of French stone. The lady, seeing such an injustice, yelled at that abusive aggressor to leave him alone, but he ignored her and tried to assault Philip again. The good thing was that others began to support the lady, managing to draw the attention of the one deceived by someone else's words because the leader had instructed him not to let Philip approach any piles of rubbish until he paid the weekly fee.

What atrocious and cruel vileness that of lying harnessed by the power to suggest people be indifferent to their fellow man, to the extent of polluting their hearts with a banal ambition for the soul.

They are innocent executioners, I believe, because they have no fault for their weakness to the pleasures that sicken them; for these weaknesses, were shaped for the purpose of being the opposite in the plan, so that the destiny planned by the Divine can be reciprocally followed; to whom nobody can appeal to their purposes or their intentions, as well as to the fortune that teaches us something that few come to understand.

All his clothes he had found in the trash, from his breeches to his hat from the thirties—all except the silver ring with a ruby in the center that his father had left him, which he jealously kept in his most valuable belongings consisting of all kinds of rare objects from different eras and for different purposes. I think a lot of collectors would love to be able to lend a hand to the trunk he kept so fondly. It was an old trunk that his father had found many years before he was born. A vestige forgotten by some galleon at the time of conquest, and that its crew charged with its purpose to the mainland, and with the passage of time somehow lasted almost intact.

In addition to his collection of mystical artifacts, which of many ignored its purpose, he also kept a collection of magazines of the _National Geographical Society_, from its first volume to the last that had been published at the time. He had many more magazines, all kinds of books, vessels, and rare objects that he snatched in his two little rooms he had built with salvaged items.

He told me that his hut was near a landslide area. I asked him if he were not afraid that something would happen, and his hut would collapse. He told me not to worry since it had been like this for many years, and nothing had ever happened. He just laughed and changed the conversation.

"Fate does not fail to let death happen in our flesh, everything will come on time," he told me.

He wore a cherry-colored bow and a very good-quality blue suit, with a violet silk shirt and wine-colored patent leather shoes, with a metal brooch. They were much older than him, you could notice, but he did not seem to care the slightest; on the contrary, he was very proud to have found that outfit so peculiar and of such good quality that he dressed it for our interview in the dark room.

"It's the Sunday, my guy," Philip told me.

I just could appreciate that nice suit, when I realize he was right. Also, he said he had found it in a pile of trash from an exclusive area of the nearest city, one day when the community's leader had gone out along with his cronies, leaving the garbage dump at everyone's mercy. Luckily, Philip was not the only one who found something that day because everyone found a lot of things with significant value, which some people used to sell to be able to buy some food. Joy grew in everyone's hearts, feeling the atmosphere as freedom. Those who found almost nothing, received from others some things so that they would not feel bad. For some did so well that they were pleased and offered to help Philip who set the initiative by sharing some things with less fortunate ones.

The day became an atmosphere of partying and celebration, where everyone cooperated with something to eat. Everything ended up in a great celebration of joy and freedom, by the absence of the oppressors who limited them. And even if it was only for that occasion, they felt truly relieved and happy.

What a pity that it had to end when the minions returned, leaving everyone quiet and not knowing what to say. They were just looking at each other as the abusive leader walked to the center of the party very angrily, with that cynical face with which he always faced them.

"Who authorized this party? I do not remember being asked. What is the big one, huh? Speak up." The only one who dared to say something was Chendo.

"We just wanted to celebrate, the birthday of some of the kids." The leader nodded and said, "All right, it's okay... Continue with your party, but tomorrow we'll talk about this."

Then he immediately withdrew with his cronies to their huts. They looked very tired. By the way, none wanted to stay to the celebration, followed their vile and voracious leader without any truce or opportunity to free themselves from their complicity, to which he had subjected them by will. A few days later then learned that they had gone to loot an archaeological excavation that was carried out near the dump, by a foreign university and the country's national university. The excavation was not secure enough to protect the finds from the ambitions of these looters, who took advantage of many objects with great historical value, relevant to our identity as a people and as for our ancestral culture. It is because of these scavengers, thieves of sacred vestiges, that those objects are known only in the black market of the upper political and social spheres, causing them to lose their value by adding the profit to it. All only for vanity and greed for power over others, which makes them selfish and petty, vile villains who rule this world.

All this indifference overwhelmed Philip in a very profound way, similar to the anguish felt by immigrants persecuted by the greed of power, to be treated as objects of exchange of interests by the most powerful nation on the planet.

At least, not everyone approves so cruel eagerness against those who build the country day by day and do not appeal to the villain's subliminal strategy. Not to his discriminatory eagerness that possesses hatred and spite, as of lack of humility and reason. They do not support indifferent madness on the part of their leader for wanting to further divide the kindness of this great nation.

The anguish of the poor is lived all over the world no matter what they have to say. If the interest of nations is not in their plans, no aid is designated for these regions. And we know that this happens today in all poor countries, where the powerful put their interests only into the resources that give them profit and control, forgetting people and denying them the necessary services for a dignified life. Violating people's rights as they often do, staying unpunished as usual.

It seems that no one can appeal to such a great sphere of political and social control; at least, so far nothing has been certain about so-called democracy, for there is no equality or social order. Much less progress in harmony and coexistence among the people who are part of that society because it seems the opposite of what these new leaders seek.

This indifference has caused outrage among those who are in favor of equality and respect for human dignity, who have worked their lives to try to raise their voices, but those voices have been quenched by the meanness of this new world order, which corrects the destiny of men according to their interest in population control to maintain their lies. For that, there is no true justice in the land of freedom, well it becomes only a false promise of laws and statutes, which the liberators offered in blood to formalize but which have been twisted by the interests of the new order.

Everyone enjoys the power of wealth and material goods, forgetting those who have the least. And in the end, it is the poor who build the walls and roofs of the indifferent rich.

Despite his miserable condition, Philip cared more about what happened to the rest of the others, no matter what he should eat for a living, or to share with his mother. Philip felt he had nothing to lose by not having much in life, and he always did favors for which he did not charge a penny; besides, the people had nothing to give him. He understood perfectly, and that is why he never expect anything in return.

He spends a lot of time lamenting the fate of everyone he knew, for that indifference that hurt many who lived the same fate as him. Sometimes he could not sleep imagining many more with his same concerns. What could he do, what could be expected? Well, always seeing suffering afflicts the soul, condemning it to the bitterness of worry, almost to the point of losing faith, hope, and the will to continue to endure such divine discrepancy. For him, it was all only divine selfishness experienced in their earthly creation. Something like that suggests that suffering is a divine decision, and is necessary to transcend. Maybe, Philip was not all wrong after all, and that is how we transcend our lives, with pain teaching us to live.

It is very profound—the wound by the abuse and indifference in the souls of the poor innocents who have the least, those who are condemned day by day by the materialistic idolatry of this *beast*, this society; in which we do not fit in with our emotions; however, we cling to it with the daily effort to get what is required, according to each other's ambition. Everyone tries to judge in their own way.

Philip had boxes full of hundreds of photos of famous artists, and lots of unopened letters. A special one from the queen of England for the president of the nation; in which, he discovered things that would show how wrong we are about some details of the history of this nation. Nobody knows how it was that such a document reached his hands, all he told me was that he had inherited it from his dad, as almost everything he possessed in those huts of laughter. He always bragged about those letters, and one time he mentioned a map of a foreign scroll, but he never gave me details of that place he mentioned as if he had already visited it. That is how he was, and that's why people rejected him in some way; well because of all that illustration in magazines and books, in every conversation with others, his expression was very profound and polite. More idealistic than anything, but enough to address any issue with anyone at any social or intellectual level. Well, all that information that he used for years, had educated him in a fluid way in almost everything. With the habit of helping without expecting anything in return, without selfishness or idolatry. That is why people around him rejected him, for that way of speaking, by commenting on issues that no one addresses when is in a pile of garbage looking for something to eat. That was him, it was not his fault, and he always helped even those who criticized him because the richness in his heart was greater than selfishness or idolatry. His work was his deeds, not his pretensions. For so, he was willing to help anyone who required his help, well it was the only thing he could give them.

He had a collection of strange things that could well be worth a fortune, but for him were his treasure, which he did not value in any monetary denomination but rather valued them in knowledge. He said had secrets for men that would torture them if they do not understand them because we were not ready for that yet, but that in due time I would have to know its contents.

They were those old vessels he kept with great zeal and never dared to open. I insisted on an occasion to tell me something about those vessels, he stop for a second and said: "You must learn to wait your time, my guy. According to your destiny, the truth will be revealed to you."

He laughed in a very honest way and without mockery of me, such that he even made me feel good and I no longer insisted on him.

At the age of three, he could read a few words, due to his mother's teachings he had from the books his dad brought him in every collection. Well, that was the only thing they let him pick up since no one wanted the books because they were not lucrative. The least the leader was interested in was literature, so they always let his dad pick up whatever he wanted from books. Managing to pile a lot of them into his hut. Also, with Philip they were the same. The leader at the time was not interested in literature in any way, so he let him pile up whatever he wanted. If he could not sell them because he thought no one would want to buy an old book. He could not comprehend the ancestral meaning of scripture in every doodle in which we tried to express the feeling of our moment. He was only interested in the material that continued to sustain him in the control of submission to others. The good thing was that he never realized that this was precisely the most dangerous weapon of submission for man. This time, ignorance played its role perfectly and did not let the villain take sides.

It was the books that filled his passion and curiosity to know more because for Philip his imagination had no limit, so he always wanted to read a new one that would give him new ideas and words to learn with his mother. She was the one who taught him good values and respect for others. The unconditional love for good learned it very well because, from a young age, his mother tried to teach him what she could. She taught him to weave and embroider, as well as to do laundry. Also taught him how to build houses with pieces of cardboard from de garbage, in which they played for hours non-stop.

They had plenty of time to share in that desolate wasteland forgotten by the hand of God.

Although they had no wealth that the world could covet, they found the unique treasure of our lives, in their moments of laughter and joy, when hunger and pain are forgotten by the joy of the soul, in the joy of the heart. At that moment nothing exists, but love. And in a moment only the memory will remain to give us the strength to move forward with what we feel, without vanity or greed, and with the absolute conviction to help without expecting something in return.

All that wisdom taught by his mother made him unique among others, a distinct individual in thought, without the notion of money, nor the cruelty of political weapons. For him, the only important thing was justice for his fellow man and solidarity with nature. Philip could have an opinion on anything commented on by people, mathematics, physics formulas, and arts. That, according to him was his passion, well Philip perfectly differentiated between the classic and the neoclassical style, the most overhanging artists of the Impressionist period and the Cubist period, In addition, to other more modern styles too. His hunger for knowledge was stronger than any greed for riches. Since greed can become a deception, he was not deceived by anyone, well he knew they were cruel and ruthless; yet he held no grudges against them, nor he was trying to blame anyone for anything but him, despite that it did not work very well that we say because he always ended up blaming the divine for the misfortune of the innocent, for their indifference and their silence.

The limited opportunities to survive in the dump, due to the abuse of the greedy executioners, left many families with no means to guarantee themselves some goods to sell and get something to eat. Some families only ate the waste they found that was still in good condition. Let us forget about the clothes, those obtained in the garbage, which was only old rags that others no longer wanted. Although, at times something good would sneak in and favor the possessor of such a find with joy.

Philip grew up in the only world in which his mother kept him for a long time until a conscious idea of the reality in which they lived was formed in him. Of the sick rose of misery and love; the incomprehensible idea of femininity and the insistent machismo trying to prove the reason. The misery exceeded his father's hopes for giving them a better life, and they were lost in unnecessary lawsuits over frustration, colliding in his mother's tears and his father's ingratitude for making her cry. For that, and for many other things, is that he never wanted to go anywhere far from the dump's area.

He did not live in a cloister or anything like that; on the contrary, he lived in the freedom that his mother always taught him, respecting nature and being gentle with others. There was no place near the dump he did not know, but not another village. Although his father tried to take him elsewhere out of the dump, he was opposed to leaving his place of conformity. There was no way to get him out of that idea. Besides, the leaders did not take much sense of his family having many privileges, so he never got out of the wretched hole they condemned his family. After the death of his mother, their hate did not change, neither compassion was felt in the villain's heart. On the contrary, they were even more cruel and ruthless. With the death of those who come together to give us life, is when we begin to miss the counsel and the incomparable affection of their intentions, the rose of their caresses, as well as that of their reprehensions; for, from them we learn our way, by their example and their dedication, and their selfless love.

The inevitable always happens, and for Philip it would be no exception, for somehow the universe conspired so he can make the right decisions for his destiny, even if he did not properly understand them, would be the decisions that would lead him to rediscover the reason why he is aware of himself, and the true path thus the immortality of the soul.

His lifelong godfather and friend, Rosendo Carrillo, whom the people called Chendo, had invited him to go to work with him on a construction site where he worked for several months, but Philip remained reluctant not to venture too far. He had developed a way of living deeply rooted in that place away from human mercy. He had already gotten used to it in such a way that he wanted nothing more for himself, well any good or wealth made him uncomfortable, and believe that what he survived and what he helped was enough. The problem was that he would no longer be alone and would have responsibilities to face, such as getting food for three instead of just the crumbs he got for himself. This time he would have a dream to fight for, without even imagining what it would mean in his spiritual life. His life would be about to turn into a tone of light that would lead others on the way to meeting their purpose.

Elida completely changed his life in a way that made him see how great the human soul can become and the miserable of its dark side. He stopped being the foreigner in his own land to become the reunifier of personal purpose, which the soul always seeks.

Despite we are in doubt of reality that does not match our true pretensions, we remain in the flow that condemns us to conformity, and we do not allow ourselves at times, to see the internal flow that could help us get out of nonconformity, without hurting anyone and without confrontations for material interests.

When Elida arrived, no one wanted her near their huts because of her appearance of had not bathed one day, with dirty dry-blooded hair and shattered rags. It was a winter solstice about noon when she suddenly appeared.

They called her the madwoman because she would sleep at the door of any hut and walk back and forth all the time. The children threw stones at her as she chased them babbling meaningless words and unable to stand at times, so she ended up on the ground at almost every step. The children made fun of her for not being able to speak or walk normally. Although the children's mothers intervened on occasions, it was just to keep them away from her, not to help her. It seemed like nobody cared. And it was precisely that, no one cared about who she was or what had brought her to such a degree of human misery.

One night, when Philip was reading a *Jehovah's Witnesses* magazine, which was concerned about the family and 'The Path That Leads to Eternal Life'. It was his hobby every night. When suddenly, he heard a noise near the entrance to his hut, but he did not pay attention to it and continued reading the contents of the magazine. He froze, lost in himself trying to understand the questions that troubled him at the time. He wondered how it was possible to live forever, how an organism could sustain itself for a considerable period; such, as forever. His knowledge of biology did not allow him to accept such a thing and he believed it was impossible for any organism to live for a longtime. It was something totally out of the reality he knew.

Cellular life on this planet has had a lot of trouble staying long. Men have managed to reach up to a hundred years or more, but with many deficiencies and almost no strength. Some plants and animals have achieved an admirable period of longevity, such as some turtles and trees, these being the longest-lived in the natural world. As some trees have lived for more than a millennium, but unfortunately like all known organisms, it is time for them to finish their cycle. Trees dry and die; and so, eternity departs far beyond what any organism can achieve, well so ephemeral is the time of its existence compared to the eternity that there is no natural possibility of such a thing as living forever.

He knew the impossible of eternal life for any organism and did not believe that such a thing was possible, much less than that would happen to him. At that moment, he came up with a revealing thought that leave him thinking about the possibility of such great madness. There is a possibility that eternal life would be achieved with offspring by reproducing us, and that is how we manage to live beyond what we can by our bones and grieving flesh. The blood of those who remain after us is what carries the purpose further, until all the living die. Then the purpose is clarified and accentuated in the spark of the one light that sustains us in eternity, our spirit.

"This would be the only way to live forever." Philip thought. Then he smiled incredulously and said quietly, "How the hell, would that happen to me?"

He was about to release a swear word, but at that moment the noise at the entrance of the hut was heard again, just before he re-leased the reproach of his mortality in the typical words of the simple man. Then he thought it was something that had fallen, some piece of wood that might have come off; for in that place, the huts fall apart with only the passage of time; or some blizzard strong enough to change their facades and leave them on the floor; or the roofs among the piles of rubbish. He did not care too much and tried to pick up the reading again.

Then suddenly, he heard a painful and overwhelming whining that made him get up immediately. He felt a chill throughout his body when he heard that desperate call for mercy and immediately went to the entrance so that he could see what it was about.

When he opened the piece of wood he used as a door in the hut, he was stunned, his eyes came out of their orbits when he saw what it was about. One could not distinguish the gender of that poor being such that his eyes saw through right at the entrance of his hut; for her condition was that of misery, even worse than his; yet he did not hesitate to try to help her.

She looked at him as he approached her with those mystical eyes that shone on him with the moonlight. He took her by the arm so he could see her face and help her from her fall. He realized that she was a young woman, almost his age, but with a degrading and miserable condition that tore his heart with a lot of feeling, which made him want to cry. He wondered how that being had come to such a condition. What an error of fate brought her to the shadow where her life was torn between indifference and ignorance from these beings lacking in mercy. How is it that she ended up asking for mercy from those who have the least? Also, how could help those who do not even have a piece of bread for themselves?

Philip's hut was on the shore of the dump through several piles of rubbish, being difficult to realize that there was someone living there, for it was the last of a few huts that were on that side of the dump.

Elida, not even finding a little mercy anywhere else, in that misery forgotten by the hand of God, wandered among those mountains of waste, desperate and hopelessness in her heart, for she had lost all strength in her body and soul such that she dropped herself in the pile like one more piece of trash; as one more waste of indifference and ingratitude, like a useless rag or a piece of dirty paper. Her body fell at the entrance of Philip's hut, where she hit her head with the wood, leaving her almost unconscious, at the precise moment when Philip was reading the *Jehovah's Witness* magazine.

Elida, falling at the entrance, motionless and unable to speak, groaned at the sky. And the few clouds that had loosened their charge upon that precise place moments before Philip opened the entrance to see what it was, they cleared, and a clearness opened by letting the moonlight pass, forming a rainbow with the rain moving away, *a rainbow in the dark.*

With the shattered heart he took her in his arms as the light faded as they entered the hut. He did not worry about closing the wood, as a sudden blizzard closed it just as they crossed the entrance. Philip just wanted to take her to a place where she could be more comfortable, and that was precisely his bed, where he dressed her and dried her with a towel that his dad had inherited him, which had an embroidered logo of the *royal family* of some kingdom of this world.

He fed her the only thing he had found that afternoon, which was just a piece of bread with a little water to soak it. By the way, that was his regular dinner that he ate in his daily reading before going to bed, but on this occasion, he did not mind losing his portion, which was very difficult for him to get at times because on some days it was only water and pieces of hard tortillas that he found. There was much misery and few opportunities for him, in that place forgotten by the hand of God. That, on many occasions, resulted in going to bed without having tasted some food for days, only water and some plants that his mother had taught him to harvest; for, she had taught him how to prepare them by combining them in a special stew so that he could eat them properly because some of them were toxic if they were not prepared with proper care and could even kill the person who consumed it.

With that food, he held for a long time, without the executioners knowing because he managed to hide them from them and their healing powers, from the strength they caused in him, and from how they nurtured it for days without eating any food other than plants. He shared this knowledge only with his godfather and lifelong friend; to whom, he asked to keep the secret so that the solicitors of lies and deceit did not know. Otherwise, they would surely take over the plants and would condemn him more to his fate of misery. And all because of the corruption of this our beloved world of greed and indifference, lacking compassion for one's neighbor; to the needy of comfort with a hunger for justice, who seeks only a slight rose of comfort that calms a little the suffering of his loneliness.

Philip had no shortage of reasons to help anyone who asked for his help, despite the unjust restrictions the executioners had on him. Therefore, they always tried to make his life impossible at all costs so that any person would have tried to flee such an unjust insistence on souring the lives of others by these meaningless creatures. The truth was, he did not want to leave others in that dark hole. He somehow sought to make their lives a little lighter with the help he offered them and thought that it would help them escape the petty control of the deceiving executioners, creating awareness in people through the example of helping each other, with selfless compassion and humility.

It is precisely all these things that most of us ignore, being the key to improving our lives is the practice of these. The heart feels it, but the obligations that society tends on our heads leave no room to seek those qualities within us.

The next morning, Elida was awakened by a ray of light passing through the wood that served as a door in the hut, and which marked the beginning of winter just as the sun came up. Philip had intentionally made it that way. Well, it was one of the many things he knew, and he used all this knowledge to make gaps all over the hut allowing it to fill with light during the day.

Philip set out to leave without realizing that she was waking up. Before he get out, a sensation on his belly stopped him and made him walk to the bed. He stayed staring at her and was unable to comprehend all that had shored this innocent and fragile being to such a miserable fate.

"You can do it," he told her.

Philip had to face the daily adventure, the unique gift that promises us a new day, and the exquisite opportunity to try it better this time, so he went to try to find something to eat, with a different reality than other days, as his thoughts changed as did his life with the arrival of Elida.

He could only bring her a piece of hard bread and a little water to soak it, which was almost what he ate during the day. Of course, that did not matter to him, and he left it near the bed for her to take it whenever she wanted.

All these gaps that he had engineered allowed the ventilation of fresh air, with the intention of keeping the hut free of mold and insects; In addition, they were useful for marking the solar shekel during the seasons. He had good and creative strategies to keep the place tidy and clean, free of bacteria and rare bugs that are among the garbage. Everything he did in an organic way, at least that is what he said; even that, on a couple of occasions he had to use a pesticide to fight the cockroaches. He always said there were no cockroaches in his house.

"If there is nothing to swallow, fewer leftovers for those wretches," said Philip remembering that moment.

There was a time when the dumpster was infested with millions of them, with no one knowing where they came from. They ate even the children's sandals and shove in their ears, for so many had to be taken to the nearest village with the doctor for throat infections, some being surgically operated on because of the cockroaches.

"Be strong, you can do it," he said, as he did every day as he said goodbye to her.

Philip left at once as she tried not to drown in her weeping. Therefore, the knot in her throat was uncovered in regenerative tears, when she was aware that he would not hear her crying. Those tears cleaned her face and gave her relief to her soul rather than to her body. She was still dehydrated and poorly nourished, without having bathed in months for wandering around for a while. Her mind was not yet entirely lucid by the blow she had received on her head, but her heart made her recognize the kindness in Philip, so she cry intensely that morning as Philip went away worrying about her, and when he brought her something to eat to bed, which he gave up so that she could sleep comfortably. Seeing this gesture of kindness so selfless and natural in him, she decided to help him with cleaning the hut while he was trying to get something to eat for both.

Days later that Elida began to take strength and Philip had to leave to get something to eat, she began to explore the place, to accommodate some things to help him a little for his attention. As she wandered moving things and shaking old, battered furniture, memories of her past came to mind that caused her such strong emotional damage that left her disillusioned about life. Sometimes she began to cry intensely as she relived the tearing of her misfortune, further hurting the wound in her heart. In those moments of anguish, she repeated herself over and over:

"How is it that I did not realize it?"

She stopped for an instant and repeated the same thing to herself.

Then after ended up checking Philip's things, even his most cherished personal belongings as she found, in the search of the clue that would give her a hint as to why he had helped her selflessly without knowing her and without judging her in any way. She has discovered something in him, which she had only seen in her mother, and would not waste her time making domestic to look at Philip's belongings to know a little more about him, and of what had prompted him to help a stranger to offer his roof, his bed and how little he could get to eat.

As she rummaged into these much-ignored treasures, she found a trunk full of papers and figurines, all sorts of rare pocket watches from different eras; in addition, a football trophy with the broken arms of the figure that resembled a player celebrating with open arms. It looked like loot from some pirate ship collecting rare objects from different parts of the world. The poems and letters represented his testimony, his sailor's diary, and his personal treasure. When opening the trunk, caught her attention the sound of a watch she found inside a box of mahogany wood with gold hardware, which it did not seem that he had opened in a good time. However, the watch worked perfectly. That intrigue her a little because she could not find a way to wind it up and did not know whether to ask Philip or not because he would find out that she was rummaging through his belongings. She had to endure until he decided to tell her about that mystery that surprised her every day, confirming that it continued to function without anyone winding it. She used it to watch the time as Philip went out and put it back before he came back.

Philip was self-taught, a jack of all trades.

He had a smaller trunk where he kept the things he used most, also some boxes full of books with different themes in each; for, he liked to study things in detail in a very meticulous and freeway, without limitations of creeds or oaths of doctrines.

In the early days, Elida had to stay awake spying on him to see if he would wind the watch, but Philip finished his night-time reading ritual and a few pages he wrote of poems and went to sleep. He wrote essays irrelevant to his condition of misery and injustice, but for him, they were a jewel, a petal of *La Rosa*.

When he fell asleep, she would fall asleep, and at dawn, she would wake up first; still, she never saw him wind it, for even the trunk did not open. Because that it was not something he really liked to do; maybe because it brought him memories that hurt him and wanted to avoid them. He did not get rid of them either because there was something he did not want to lose, something physical that we keep as a memory of the beings we love most in life. Such were the memories of his parents that fed and tormented him at the same time, keeping him between pain and joy.

In the letters Elida found from Philip's father to his mother, she realized that they had not been happy. This affected her in such a way that she prayed for her on some occasions of the day, so she might have light in her walk to her new spiritual stage.

After a few days, she noticed a leather bag that was inside the trunk. To her surprise, it was Philip's mother's purse, and inside was her diary detailing all the moments of her life, as well as her truncated dreams and her sincere desires. Elida took it and read it carefully, and on every page, she read, understood a little more of the suffering of that woman who had to shut up for a long time, without anyone knowing or caring about her dreams or her dignity. When she realized she was not the only one to have lost faith and hope, cried intensely with great feeling. For, she could not believe how indifferent the world of men has become to the beings who give us life. That is vile and rude, hurting another being by confusion of conflict and self-indifference.

In some ways, we were hurting others with our actions or with something we said at a certain time of insanity or stupidity; those that happen very often in the lives of all of us. Some of us had the will to accept our mistakes, so we broke the ego to accept guilt. Despite we do not try it in any way with treachery; and maybe, without wanting to hurt or offend, we hurt others with our words.

"I did not want to hurt you, but my reality pushed me," Philip said as we debated the moment; for so, I thought that because of his personal experiences and mine, he was somewhat right. Everyone passes judgment on their own.

They introduced each other on the third day that she awoke from her lethargy of suffering. For, by losing faith in life, the soul suffers from great sorrow. He approached her as she continued in the bed almost covering up half of her face, he could only see her eyes and her tousled hair. He stared at her until he got close to her.

"Philip Adame Alvarez. That is my name."

She was silent knowing his name, wanting to cry but she held on and only stared at him. Philip left right away, after telling her what he always told her every morning.

"Be strong, you can do it."

Philip walked to the door.

"Elida Almaraz Nájera, my name is Elida," she told him, with a sweet and tender voice that made him stop immediately. He turned and watched her sitting on the bed, now able to see her face and identify her voice. Philip was with a smile that broke his face into two hemispheres of joy, which increases his heart rate, and struggled to breathe when he saw her. Well, he felt a strange sensation in his stomach when he saw her eyes, and to feel that she was there near him.

"Nice to meet you," they both said at the same time.

"All right, you can do it," Philip told her. "I will come back later."He went out on his personal adventure, to that reality that keeps him busy without realizing who he is in life. As if that were the purpose, keeping you busy, as a distraction from what really happens behind the smokescreen that forms the lies, of those who govern people's tastes and fashions; as well, as what should be eaten, and how it should be dressed in every particular social and economic class.

Of course, cultural heritage is important in every region, but in the end, they do not separate from the globalization of the means of control used to manipulate the democracy and decency of societies in our reality.

Today no nation or country is freed from political, religious, or social conflicts. Everywhere we have differences, moral and existential divisions such that we were never as divided as now in what is right for everyone and what is right for some.

The manipulations have been successful, and that is why there is an idea of racial division in some men in the nations of this world because of the misunderstanding of their personal details. They have let themselves be carried away by the current of noise that pollutes their mind with garbage, leaving no room for themselves.

We take care of everything but ourselves. We want justice and peace; however, that is not what happens today. On the contrary, we get carried away by the words of others and the ideas that make us feel emotionally identified. The common good is not sought, only economic, political, and religious interests that only bring more confusion to the external noise. We do not live by helping our neighbors, but we always live by marginalizing the poorest and most needy.

This debated Philip with me as he told me his most sincere personal secrets, as well as his knowledge of what many of us do not know in everyday life, for reasons that everyone has personally, but which will recognize in themselves. Those details that we ignore, the ones we let go unnoticed by the outside noise of the events that occur in that reality that we ourselves have formed, are the experience that would help us to understand ourselves first, rather than judging others by our mistakes. There is a clue to every being who wants to, whoever is interested in deciphering these details.

Every day they talked more, to the degree of chatting every night late about topics that many people would find a mere stupidity, a waste of time, but for them, it was a great amazed to discover that they perfectly got along with each other, and what people might think did not matter to them. They laughed and cared for the ideas they said as if they wanted to change the world together with justice and truth.

She had a profile of a very well-prepared and educated person, unlike him, who was a filthy uprooted man who did not care or how his hair looked, who always made a fuss and without combing.

"It's style," Philip said when referring to his hair.

Still, they got along very well. She found relief in the talks they held on to every night when he came back from getting something to eat.

In this way, they met, in that forgotten place far from the mercy of man and social justice. Despite that beggar and mad appearance, Elida had been very well educated. Philip realized this when he chatted with her, but he did not ask her anything personal because he wanted her to be the one who decided to tell him what she wanted, so as not to bother her with what he might ask her, well she was still stunned by everything that had happened to her, and she was not in the mood to corrupt the good coexistence they had with her bitter past; therefore, she decided to tell him after a while after there was better trust between them. Though she trusted him in a good way, it takes time to let go of our bitterness at times. It is not easy to trust everyone after you have been betrayed by those you blindly trusted.

Elida, as in every day Philip went out, set to improve the place to the extent that she could. She set out to improve the rainwater collection system Philip had invented. It was not that the system was wrong, but it required some improvements to work perfectly. That is why she worked every day to improve it more and more.

There were some containers that Philip used to store the water rain but had no filtration for human consumption. Between the two containers Philip engineered, Elida put a small container halfway with sand, and the other half stuffed with a pile of charcoal She put together the containers with some plastic hoses so the water can be filtered. Philip boiled the water they drank to sterilize it from any bacteria, but with Elida's improvement to the collection system, they would also avoid the dangerous metals in the rainwater; for the air is no longer clean today and pollutes the rain, and when falling to the ground affects plants and every living being that tries to survive among our selfishness; among our voracious vanity for the consumption of resources that is inconsiderately made around the world.

Chapter 2
The Gargoyle and the Medallion

One day a sandstorm razed through the dump almost changing its place, leaving the huts almost bare bones. It came like this, suddenly just at sunrise. Nobody thought to even prepare a little because it caught them asleep.

Even though some had already woken up, there were many who slept still, and they did not have even time to put on a flip flop. The roaring noise of the wind crashing the battered huts, falling apart almost entirely, awakened them terrified, screaming for forgiveness to heaven, and weeping heartbrokenly believing that this was their end. They thought God had decided to judge them, to pay for the blame and transgressions they had committed against their fellow man during their lives.

The sand was tucked through their eyes and through their ears, being deaf, blind, and without knowing for sure what was really going on. The children hugged their mothers and mothers protected their children, while some parents were trying to keep up the little that was left to protect them. That scary wind left the dump almost clean of garbage, except for the sticks left over from the huts, and a few belongings that survived to those poor beggars, which was almost nothing.

By the time the huts were about to collapse the storm passed, and everyone was dismayed, looking scared. You could hear some children and women crying out of the scare, terrified. Arguably, some men could not contain their sanity and wept for their faults, for the pain they might cause at some point of insanity to an innocent being, for their own conscience judged them, they could not deny such guilt.

There was a child who said, during the uncertainty, that God had spoken to him to tell them a message, but with the confusion and crying, no one paid any attention to that poor infant who did not cry or complain about what had happened. He did not look dirty with any sand, as strange as it may seem. One of the elders who lived there saw him in the middle of a swirl of air protecting him from the sand. There was no explanation for how that was possible, and he wondered what mighty force took sides among these men that the world marginalized with their indifference.

The elder was one of the last native priests of that land, advising those who sought him knowing his counsel and wisdom, but for the rest of the others was just an old indigenous beggar, of whom no one cares what he had to say because he could only speak few words in their language. Besides being an old man, and the old people are ignored today their advice, which even their relatives do not seek, but they condemn them to an asylum of strangers, so they can live their days in their own way, forgetting their warmth of love that welcomed them when they were kids.

Sustained only from his cane, the old man freed himself from the storm by the favor of some strange force that somehow works among us, as in the rest of those who survived that day in that place, where only the frightened and dusty faces of the people were left looking at each other, even within where their huts were supposed to remain.

When the boy tried to tell them what he had experienced, the old man looked at him uttering a few words in his native language, while he was on his knees pointing the cane at the child. Confusion and fear gripped everyone ignoring the old man and the child with the message.

They are not guilty, nor is it a punishment from the divine, it is a lesson that each will have to discover by itself, in the way that the spirit has taken on this ground; formed from the dust of our bones and the walk of our grieving flesh. In our daily work, with the actions we take and the words we say to our fellow man. Everyone judge by yourself why indifference confuse us, as to act against nature, which feeds us with its fruit branches.

Suddenly the sun came up, welcoming them a little with its heavenly warmth. It was then that they realized they were still alive. They looked at their bodies and their faces squirted with tears the dread stopped by only a few whining of the children. Some men and women covered their private parts with what they found near them; at least with what little was left, which were just a few old rags. Anyway, it was enough to cover themselves sufficiently in a decent way. For the loss was very tragic for some of those wretched, who in case they had almost nothing.

Philip and Elida had fallen asleep late the last night in one of their evening talks because they could not come to a reasonable conclusion for both on a topic they discussed.

Already late, they decided to go to sleep and left the subject for another time, after the two gathered more evidence for their arguments in their evening debate.

For some strange reason, Philip's hut had not suffered much damage compared to the devastation it made with the other huts.

Elida awoke to a whisper in her ear that told her the same words the child tried to say to people after the storm. Elida opened her eyes, and she could hear some screams. She got up and ran to wake up Philip who was sleeping in a small hammock. Pale and scared faced he was still sleeping, trembling and moving from side to side babbling meaningless words. Elida had to push him to wake him up, and he fell to the ground but rose immediately, he was staring at her sensing what was going on. At the time she told him that something had happened outside and that they better go to see what it was.

"No, it can't be true, the people, the people," he said as he ran out to see what had happened.

Elida, as she could take some rags that had been given to her and came out after Philip with that feminine intuition that is inherited from high where the purest spirits dwell, and that is reflected in maternal foreboding more than in any other feeling in the living.

On his way out, Philip was astonished at the desolation by the misfortune of some unfortunate ones who had lost everything, standing still for an instant by the impression. Long enough for Elida to catch up with the rags in her hands running non-stop to the huts of some women who were left without much covering their bodies. Philip followed her to try to help those poor people who cried for some mercy; by the misfortune that had fallen upon them. To such an extent that he did not know who to help first, well everyone was crying for help.

Some needed clothes to cover their shame, others needed hope, which they had lost when they felt close to death. A little pity or a word of encouragement, anything would be of great use in that moment of misfortune.

Suddenly, they stumbled between going from one hut to another, just for a few seconds, almost just to cross sights. Philip touched her on her left shoulder with his right hand, and she with both hands touched him on his chest right in his heart, then ran to help anyone they could. It did not take long to match in their neighbor's hut. They were good friends since they were little and lived there with his wife and three children. Their hut had not suffered much considerable damage either, for that strange force that comes without anyone noticing how or where it manifests, or why some are graced in a certain way and others are not.

They were found inside the hut without knowing what to do, desperate because they could not find the youngest of the three children. The biggest of the children was the one who opened the door for them because the lady had a nervous breakdown, and the husband was trying to comfort her. As soon as Elida and Philip entered the hut, the boy ran in behind them straight to hug his mother. She jumped with joy at seeing him, not letting the child say a word, but the boy got away as he could from her frenetic kisses and said: "Don't worry Carmela, I'm fine. Remember that I love you very much, I won't leave you, I won't go, but there are others outside who need you."

The words of that six-year-old boy took a great strength in the mother, for she took him kissing his cheeks with a big hug, then left him with the other two children, and then they went to help others in what could be done. Each couple opted for a different course so that they can go to more places at the same time. They ran from place to place to provide their help with a firm disposition and without any social or political prejudice. They did not hesitate to come immediately to help in whatever their hands and breath were possible, for the words of relief they could give them were of great help to their sadness.

Philip's mind flew within his reproaches, at the same time he thought about how good this was to people if anyone can see it that way.

Philip believed that, in a way, it was a message of purification for the soul of all those who were so misled. Philip knew that not only material pollutes the spirit, but also the confused noise of society that we maintain every day, by following the goals defined in the model of goods, fame, and prestige. This created greed for money, just to seek luxuries we do not need, ending up many in the trash can.

This kind of reproach left Philip with a sensation of unconformity, as to why some suffered more than others, or why the rich had a better condition to survive than the poorest. If these are the ones who keep the coffers of the powerful full, the builders of their castles, who bring food to everyone's mouth and clean up the dirt that others pollute.

Some huts were not damaged as much as others that were left in the pure sticks of the corners, which held the few pieces that covered the walls.

From the less damaged huts came people out to help others who were not as lucky as them. As they were safe and in a better condition of giving a hand, they joined others in solidarity, well Elida and Philip had infected them with their intention to help. This act of mercy to those less in grace became the lightest burden for them, still, they did not rest until they saw that everyone was okay.

That was one of those days on which the freshness of the new dawn was not felt that morning feeling of renewal and hope. Maybe, the hope was lost at the time of feeling death near, but it renewed the old prejudices and tested the faults of each one in some way. Well, by judging themselves, they pleaded guilty to whatever happened to them at the time. Some understood that they were wrong in what they did, or in what they said on a certain occasion against some person or nature; for so, some regretted the bad they did, and then now they knew how to avoid it next time because they learned from their own mistakes details that they might have avoided. The same way it might occur to any of us, at the time they did not understand it and ended up getting carried away by the passion of emotions. That way, by repenting of the bad, they cleansed their guilt by renewing them with good intentions.

Hope returned to their hearts as the minutes passed, and the sun warmed their poor, semi-naked unprotected, and vulnerable bodies to any disease that the scare might cause them. So, if your soul decays, your body is also unprotected against disease.

There was a hut in the middle of the dump that had a rectangular white stone just in front of the entrance, aligned at sunrise and pointing westward. Philip hurried to go to see if anyone needed help in that place because he knew of the old man who lived there and thought something had happened to him. A sudden thought came to him that disturbed him in such a way that he ran away immediately. Similarly, Elida had felt it at the same instant and ran out to that old man's hut to see what had happened to him.

As they approached, a whining was heard from the old Suzeo's hut, which was what everyone called him. Elida went immediately inside as soon as she got there. Philip entered right behind her, when she approached the old man slowly, not knowing what to do, a little frightened by the scene that was before her eyes. The old man was lying on the ground with a gargoyle of more than two meters on top of him. For what strange reason it may seem, the stone gargoyle held the old man's hands against the ground, while the left horn of its head was fitted in the old man's chest. This reptile-type gargoyle with bull horns seemed very real. Besides, the position that it was at the top of the old man gave much to think about, which was why Elida did not know what to do. The old man stared at her, in agony trying to say something, but his words did not make sense. How could, after all, a horn have pierced his chest? She came close enough to touch the old man's forehead and tell him to be strong, but he knew he would not survive that. The old man was dying while he was trying to tell her something, so Elida insisted he not move, but the old man knew that was his end, for he used his last breath to tell her: "She is alive." Old Suzeo died while Elida touched his forehead.

Elida entered a nervous breakdown, by the old man's words, filling her with great confusion. To such an extent that she stood still not knowing what to think. If not for Philip who was behind her, she would have lost her sanity or something.

Philip hugged her and told her that there was nothing to do for him, at least in this life. Both noticed a medallion that the old man had on top of him as if the gargoyle had dropped at the time of fitting the horn to his chest. Elida took it and put it in her purse, immediately so that no one could see it because it was something that did not fit in that place. This magnificent jewel, with stones that seemed to have its own light, did not seem to be from this time; besides it was no place for such a thing as that in the dump.

Elida knew that such a jewel did not belong there, also she felt that not even to this world because the light that the stones emanated was not very common to the stones from this planet; at least, she had never seen anything like it. It was something that seemed to be worthy of a king, or of a God because there was no reason for that jewel to be there, and she wondered how it had come to that very insignificant place, where no one seemed worthy of such a thing. Elida pulled it out of her purse and gave it to Philip, who put it on immediately and covered it with his rags so no one could see it. Philip felt something strange about that relic such that it made him think that might have some clue that would clarify what really happened on that occasion. Some about the mystery to which old Suzeo referred to what he had said, about the nature of that mysterious stone gargoyle.

The few who dared to approach were terrified to see the poor, lifeless bloodied old man lying beneath the gargoyle. His twelve-year-old granddaughter and his thirty-three-year-old son rushed into the hut to help their loved one. That desperate man immediately tried to lift the gargoyle on his own, but all he managed to do was further aggravate the crying he had in a cry of fury, of pain to see his father in that mortal condition. Philip tried to lift it by himself that beast made of stone, so immediately others joined him, and together they were able to lift the gargoyle enough to release the old man. They were several men full of precise strength to achieve such a thing. That man son of old Suzeo was devastated in a great way that, they all let go of the weeping after hearing the bitterness of his pain. Understanding in themselves the pain of losing a loved one, they did not hesitate to help him with his sorrow, by freeing his father from the horn of the beast that had taken his life.

That man tormented by the decision of the divinity, and whose name was Manuel, took his father in his arms to take him to a more dignified place in front of his hut, which was a white stone in which the old man sat every day to appreciate the sunset, likewise in the same stone was the first to receive the day when the sun rose. What a tragic coincidence, what signs of the end bring our destiny.

The community leader, seeing the old man wrapped with white sheets that they had covered him with, ran out shouting, "No, it cannot be!"

And moving away as quickly as possible while still turning back with his gaze fixed on the old man, who was dead on top of the white stone. This coward was trying to escape from his fears instead of confronting them, well he also had faults to redeem on his conscience. He was an ignorant selfish, spoiled child, who never accepted his mistakes and neither allowed advice from anybody about what he wanted to do or was planning to do. He never apologized for his pranks, much less for his disrespect, to those who he made suffer.

Fleeing from our own faults is foolish and ignorant. Maybe, confronting our mistakes, our faults, is how we move one more step towards reunion with our personal purpose if it is the case that the spirit must learn anything else.

It was the only death claimed by that incident, despite having left several with nothing, which was almost all they had. It only took one soul from the living, old Suzeo.

At the age of seventy-two gave up his carnal life in the hands of matter to continue in his flowering shekel on the ground, which formed from the bones and flesh of those who left before us. His spirit transcended spiritual knowledge as he passed the threshold of life in his carnal death. Realizing some things when he was still alive, he learned things that have been excluded from every man's basic education; that is spiritual education. Not the education of institutions with doctrines that appear to be good, nor radical separatist beliefs of ideas that only form prejudices and role models based on machined objectives. It could be that this is what keeps us stunned. We live imprisoned without realizing it.

All this external noise generated by our daily duties sometimes does not let us hear our inner voice, which is wanting to release a little reason in our thoughts as earthly men. Not everything is wrong, but it may be that there is something that we have not considered, being that what spoils the dream model of peace and love for all of us who live on the planet. Everyone judges for themselves.

What a coincidence of fate, for the old man had found it one night of the new moon. That night, the utility workers who were digging a hole to put more rubbish had left early that day, due to a national strike from the union. The workers opposed the miserable wages that the government misused, which was why they decided not to do anything with their hands, and showed the power of their decisions, organizing a national strike to claim their rights.

Nor working, not doing everything required for the system to survive; only so, was how they managed to become aware of those who have petty power, those who seek only political and monetary interests. Not agreeing with the lack of appreciation and not being silent, is how they conquer better wages, besides other decent benefits.

The old Suzeo had already heard of the strikes by the unions and even attended a meeting to protest in the nearby village along with other more people who had nothing to do with the matter, but who were paid for by others with interests opposed to those who dominated the union administration. They were offered a ham cake and a fifth, which they accepted without hesitation. After receiving their payment, they left immediately to shout the suggestion by the vulgar vice of corruption with their petty interests, which have nothing to do with the social good, and bring no benefit or progress to the people.

The old man waited for them to leave to find out if he could find anything useful among the workers' machines, or something personal that they had forgotten. Well, for people who live in that place, anything is good to sell or pawn, so that they can procure some bread and be able to live one more day in misery.

Often, the conditions push us to commit the unthinkable in order to continue living in the comfort and relief of certain responsibilities. With money being the main means for the peace of mind of such responsibilities or obligations, such as mortgage payment, or the electric bill. For those who live here, the unique concern is to eat at least once a day, otherwise they know that there is no opportunity on the part of governments to help with some fair program that will help them progress. Something to improve their conditions, with health services and education. For so, is that these deceived ones have no hope, for the null intention of politics for the social good because of interests that deceive many with their words, which brings no benefit, just hate and quarrels of existentialist ideas that only divide.

The thief must be punished regardless of his social affiliation, how much money he has or because he does not have goods that guarantee a sustainable value in society.

Some machines remained there, so old Suzeo ventured down the side of the hole, on the side where there was almost no light; so that no one could see him come down.

Being halfway there, by the eagerness to see what he might find, he slipped falling about three meters, but suddenly became hooked by the horn of the gargoyle that oversized the hillside, preventing him from falling to certain death on some stones that were in the bottom. He recovered from the fright and realized that that strange face of the horned lizard had saved his life. When he realized the mystery of the little exposed on the downhill, he immediately started to dig around the head to find out what it was about. When he had uncovered its neck, he could see something shiny that seemed of great value, but that was attached to the gargoyle and there was no way that he could remove it with his hands; for that, he decided to go and warn the community leader of his find.

That was the same medallion that the old man had on his neck when Elida and Philip found him about to die because of the wound that had caused him the horn of that stone statue. But when the old man found it, it was stuck to the gargoyle.

"How was that possible?" Philip wondered, seeing him lying on the white stone wrapped among white sheets, and a red overflow that Elida put on him to cover his wounds.

These wounds had apparently been made by the claws of the gargoyle, according to the marks on his chest as well as the blood on the beast's claws.

From one of the arms was that the old man carried the beast after it was pulled out of the hole, without almost anyone noticing what was going on. Only the leader's henchmen who always helped him plunder. Dragging it by nine men took it to the leader's house. But the old man and the leader returned leaving the others cleaning the gargoyle; for the old man had noticed something else that had been left in the place of the find. They did not let anyone near, among a pile of rags they pulled out something else that they soon tried to hide quickly.

Philip's father had told him the story of the gargoyle when he was a child, a time before he had to leave. Somehow, so to speak, on the same path as fate showed Philip every day when he discovered the purpose for which he lived.

He told him that, he had seen with his own eyes that beast with horns and reptile face, besides what the leader had hidden, and that he made Philip swear that he would never say anything about it because his life would be in danger. But Philip was only a child believing that it was only another fable that his father told him to entertain him while watching the sunset together. That was the reason he never took any importance of it until he looked at the old man under the gargoyle with the medallion around his neck and see him lying lifeless on the white rock.

His father told him that it had been put in the warehouse that the leader used to wait for the things he took from the community, in addition to what was always stolen from archaeological excavations near that region.

The old man's hut was located under that warehouse where the thieves kept their great treasure. The old Suzeo was something like the guard of that vault that kept great mysteries. The leader had a small room built by his cronies on top of where the old man's hut was so that no one could ever see the gargoyle. Well, the old man never allowed any person to pass from the door of his hut, and never walked away from it. Only went from the hut to the stone at dawn, with the same ritual at sunset. His son and granddaughter were the only ones who came out of the hut, but only to look for something to eat, being the ones who fed and cared for him.

The only ones who were with the old man, besides Elida and Philip, at the time of leaving the body and transcending to the spiritual world, were his son and granddaughter, in addition to a few others, as many were still very hurt from having lost their huts along with how little they had. They were stunned even by the sandstorm and were unable to attend to the pain of those who had lost their loved ones. Their misfortune prevented them from seeing the misfortune of the other. At least in some because Elida and Philip together with others did not hesitate to help in what they could. They stayed with that man and the girl until the Red Cross arrived, along with two municipal officers to offer them help.

Two nurses and a nun who came in with them immediately went to help people in whatever was necessary. To their surprise, there were people who piled up to ask for some help. They gave some people something to eat and attended to some minor fractures, among some small wounds that were nothing but scratches; likewise, they were treated as if they were mortal wounds with all kindness and care.

One of the officers questioned the witnesses, with Elida being first on his list, who hesitated to tell him about the gargoyle. She told him that she had found the dead old man under some debris that had fallen due to the storm; for which the officer asked them to show him the location of the accident. Elida pointed to the old man's hut, and now Philip stared at her. The officer noticed his gaze, then Philip turned to the hut without the officer taking his eyes off him. When Philip turned to see the officer again, the officer stood thinking a little before deciding to enter the hut. No one followed him.

He stopped at the entrance for a few seconds, and he entered the hut slowly to find out what had happened.

According to his observations, he deduced that the warehouse floor had fallen because something fell on the roof, broke the sticks holding it, and fell right next to where old Suzeo slept. He was able to notice by the blood in some of the wood that fell that the old man had died for that cause. Strangely, he found no sign of the gargoyle, it had vanished from the scene without anyone having noticed.

It was not possible that they had moved it so quickly. Something mysterious happened because it was too heavy a piece. Besides in the old man's hut, there was only one entrance, it was not possible for them to take it out without them noticing. After a few minutes, the officer came out very calm and relaxed without showing any impression of what he had seen because he was not entirely surprised or immediately asked about the gargoyle. He wrote something down in his notebook very sure of his conclusion, while Philip and Elida looked at him with uncertainty because the officer never asked them about the gargoyle. They in turn did not mention it, like everyone who helped move it to get the old man's body stuck in the beast's horn. Neither the granddaughter nor the old man's son said a word.

The officer stared Philip in the eye, but Philip did not move or doubt at all. He turned to see Elida, and she turned to look at him also carefully.

He approached her a little, took off his cap with the badges he was wearing, and said, "You were right, miss, the debris took the poor old man's life," as he looked at the body of the old man who laid on the stone.

Philip and Elida did not understand what happened, so they kept seeing each other for an instant. Then, both at the same time decided to enter the hut to check with their eyes the reason why the officer did not ask them anything about it. The same scene that the officer saw, they saw also inside the hut. Without explaining what could have happened with the gargoyle, nor because many things had suddenly changed. They saw with their eyes what had happened to the old man, among others more besides them, but they said nothing, though they had seen the same thing as Philip and Elida. She hugged him feeling a little afraid, so Philip took her in his arms and told her not to fear, that everything was going to be okay.

While the officer was watching the scene of the devastation left by the storm, the other officer and two monks took care of the body to investigate the nature of the wounds and what might have caused them. But the old man only had a large purple spot on the chest, with a little blood at shoulder height, which came from the fracture of some fingers on both hands. It seemed as if he had tried to take off something that had fallen on him, and trying to free himself from it, fractured his hands with it. The object broke the roof, as well as the warehouse floor just below where the old man was, falling on top of his body and his wretched luck, taking his life at the time; at least that was the conclusion of the officers from sharing the evidence they had obtained separately.

The officers decided to take the body to the nearest town for an autopsy and asked for his son and granddaughter to accompany them, which they accepted peacefully.

After a few hours of helping and feeding those they needed most, they made sure that each and everyone, including children, will take a white pill that, according to them, it would help them against infections.

Philip, taking advantage of the body being raised in one of the vans to take him to the village morgue, took Elida to his hut to lie down a little, well she had turned somewhat pale by the impression of what had happened. Philip did it to prevent them from being forced to take the pill, as it did not give him much confidence, because of a strange feeling he felt in his chest, making him act immediately to slip away from them.

In order to make sure everyone took the pill, the officer went to Philip's hut, as if he had noticed where they had gone, to ask them in person to take it. He did not leave until he looked at them putting it in their mouth by the insistence of the officer because Philip had told him that he would take it later, but the officer insisted, having no choice but to take it. When he saw them swallow it with a little water, the officer was pleased and said goodbye saying,

"Have you guys one pleasant day, excuse me." And with that, he turned to leave.

"Same for you," said both at the same time.

Philip, as soon as the officer left the hut, said to Elida, "Don't take it."

Wanting to get the pill out of her mouth with his hands. She had not swallowed it, spit it out as she looked at him wondering if she had swallowed it. Philip had spit it out too just as she did. Feeling calm that she had not swallowed it, he embraced her tightly. Elida, sensing Philip's concern, took refuge in his arms, in his heart; of which she fell increasingly in love for his simplicity and nobility, in addition to his selfless intention to help without grief to whoever asked.

As the days passed, people recovered little from that misfortune, thanks to the rubbish that came from the nearby villages, for from this came the materials to rebuild the huts, along with things that could be sold to procure some food— these being that the only thing those poor people could expect, the rubbish to rebuild their lives.

Philip and Elida, in their evening talks, debated any logical possibility of what might have happened that day, using every detail based only on the logical reason of reality, without touching the possibility of fantasy because that seemed to them a mere fantasy, and they didn't want to accept that that happened, at least the way they saw it. The talks were revealed many nights during that time of reconstruction, both physical and moral. That time was enough for everyone to take hold of the dump.

Hope changed some for the better because they repented from the heart of their evil deeds and dedicated themselves to doing good in the way the heart guided them. Others did not care and continued their misunderstanding with others as before the tragedy. As they no longer felt death or punishment about their guilts, they remained indifferent to the pain of others, regardless of what might happen to them as a result of their cruelty, and ignored the lesson with that indifference.

That fear that changed many and condemned some in their own personal hell, according to their conscience, made them forget the choice of the spirit and its missions in the carnal life. Philip suspected the silence of the people regarding the old man and his relatives, well no one said anything again since that day of the storm. For some strange reason, Elida and Philip were the only ones who remembered him every night in their night debates, where they used logic to continue to deny the absurd. But Elida no longer refused the truth of her conscience, telling Philip in a night months later, of what had happened in that bitter awakening:

"He said she was alive. Besides, I saw when you and those guys moved that beast to free him. You've seen it with your own eyes. That this happens to me all the time so much that I've been crazy. Please, what is it? If you are bent on denying it, even that ye have seen the truth, then you are foolish." Philip smiled a little at how candid her accent seemed to him, which she had inherited from her grandparents.

He interrupted her with a strong embrace stopping her annoyance for denying the facts with insufficient logic, which only confuses men. With a tender look without any worldly greed for wealth or fame, he looked into her eyes saying:

"I believe you. I saw it too, didn't I? Time will tell, don't worry." Elida let go of the cry as she recalled her father's words in Philip's, as well as the warmth of security on his chest, which made her feel things from her past that she had forgotten, for that tragedy that took her to the entrance of Philip's hut, and that kept her for many months without remembering who she really was. It is possible that people did not want to talk about what had happened that day, for with their personal tragedies they had forgotten the old man's. Maybe, Philip and Elida remembered everything that happened because they had not taken the pill. Who knows.

Chapter 3
The Old Lady with the White Hair

The unconditional love she always showed to all being rosing her feelings, gave her a great reputation with all who knew her up close.

They knew very well of her simplicity of open heart, of those hearts that give without expecting any personal benefit. For this reason, everyone respected her for the great act of service she was doing to anyone who asked her to do so. Elida appeared when they needed it most when misfortune took them by surprise. As they were grieving, she healed them with great affection and respect; for that reason, many regretted having treated her badly when she recently appeared in the dump. She shook hands with them without any grudge, without reproach or demand, only in the interest of giving and helping all that poor being who needed her help.

Philip was pleased to have found someone so close to his principles and customs that all he did good in the day was to think of her. She admired Philip's personality with great tenderness and respect for the way he had offered her what little he had, without even knowing who she was. That made Elida sees the true being who lived inside Philip's body.

Elida took time to adapt to the customs that people quietly agreed to, for fear that the leaders would intimidate them with their threats of restriction, of who could and who could not access the piles of garbage that came from better places; So that was the way they controlled the population. With the plan of the chief leader of those who could collect the best garbage, everyone's participation was guaranteed according to the rules that he imposed for his own benefit. Without anyone ever openly complaining.

To keep them a little happy, the leader rotated them in shifts so that those who paid the required fee would collect the best piles of garbage. He kept them with some hope so that they would continue to want to emerge from their imaginary misfortune, but without the means to grow spiritually.

All material is available to man's hands to satisfy the ego and vanity, but for the spirit, not enough time has been allowed, in the time that has been imposed on the obligations, on the model that this society demands from all those who make it up.

The means that make it easier for men to grow spiritually fades among the lies of the leaders, which have been suggested by an ancient force that controls them without remedying their personal causes. They are somehow slaves too, for the power given by the hand of the highest of these, controls them with evil pleasures of eternal promises. Some know nothing, they are puppets of others that belong to a higher circle, which are only allowed to ascend by design.

The lack of will from the majority in the dump to appeal to the unfair rules imposed on them filled Elida with great concern, who commented on it very often in her evening debates with Philip. On one occasion Philip told her:

"Customs that people adopted out of fear and ignorance. Always has been like this.""They have no choice, no worthy opportunity. That's why their hopes are dying," Elida said.

Philip was proud to hear her say that because of the passion with which she cared about children and the way she understood the situation. With a great hunger for justice for those whom society condemned to the lowest. Elida realized that the children were not going to any school, for there had never been one in that place forgotten by the hand of God. The parents did not have time to teach them to read and write to their children because they spend all day recycling and trying to sell what little they could find amid the garbage; besides, they themselves could not read or write.

What could they do, when all they could get was to eat that day, or for a few days? Some worked to hide things of significant value so that the officers of the leaders would not notice. Those bitch buddies who took advantage of all the people being cruel despots, double-sided hypocrites. When they lived with people without the leader's command, they were candid, but they were cruel under his command. The leader also controlled them with rewards of goods and pleasures that they could enjoy, such as doing almost no more work than supervising to make everything work according to his orders. In this way, the leader could have closer everyone the whip to frighten them so as to punish anyone who tried to break the law; for everyone should comply with it according to his petty decree, or else they would suffer the punishments of the abusers.

One night they debated the law and the responsibility that man has in fulfilling that agreement which he has cordially accepted in the commitment to society that encompasses not only the earthly but the divine as well. She suggested that any law given to men would corrupt it in any way if that law limits their earthly interests.

"See that it was said it by the greatest of all, that loving oneself comes first, then your neighbor," Elida told him.

Philip stared at her with great satisfaction feeling great pride in the way she perceived reality. To contribute to her personal epiphany, he aggregated:

"Perhaps that is the only law to be followed, and then no law is necessary, for love is the one that governs, and love does not hurt." She stared at him in the same way as he did with her, with great admiration; for which Elida said:

"The free of the soul: Love." Their faces turned red without knowing what to say afterwards because they felt their hearts coming out of their chests, and their breath was cut off.

He got up from where he was sitting for not holding what he felt and went for some water to run away from the moment, as she said in low voice, at the moment when he was moving away from her, "I can't hold it on," he realized, but he shut up and decided to do nothing because he felt it was not the time.

In the end, they went to sleep and let fate work their indecisions for them.

Some adults taught their children some things like some principles of math, reading, and writing, among other things they kept secret only among the family. They were doing so out of fear of reprisals from leaders, or for some family creed they had inherited to protect themselves from abusers. Philip did not know many things that had happened in that region long before he was born; as well, as he also did not know about others who read among the garbage community.

Philip thought he was the only one, but there were others among them their grandparents had taught them some things that people commonly ignore. These are those who learned from the Jesuits who once passed through that place a long time ago when the most enlightened minds of royalty excused themselves in the conquest and sought insistently the remnants of truth.

Gradually Elida became aware of the health conditions in which children were growing up, their lack of education about good customs, and the lack of opportunity that people commonly have in the poorest places on this planet. Elida felt there was no hope for the children because there had never been a school in that place. The nearest one was three-and-a-half to four hours on foot; in addition, it was a very precarious school that did not have the basic services to house many students. There were only a few rooms made of adobe, with roofs of sticks and curls with dirt on top. It had only one teacher for the few children in that town who attended to learn primary education.

This greatly dismayed her such that in the evenings when Philip watched the sunset as he returned from his search routine among the garbage, she sat next to him dreaming of a way to help those poor innocents who had to start collecting at the age of six, just like as their parents and grandparents had done since the dump had been founded.

There were two neighbors who had taken a great affection for her simplicity and innocence, who always sought her after Philip left in the mornings. These became her pimps and confidants in everything that has to do with the life of a woman, who came to see them as her family, for all the good things they did for her. They had a habit of braiding each other's hair, thanks to the magazines Philip had with different types of hairstyles from different countries, with step-by-step illustrated details. They stained their hair with cosmetics found in the trash, without thinking about the side effects in order to look attractive.

Her pimps gave her clean clothes and red sheets in a new unopened package, to be released at night when her man returned from his day, according to the insinuations of her pimps. So, she would somehow understand the natural encounter between man and woman, yielding to what fate had already indicated. She knew it but could not find the right time to prove it to him. Somehow, she did so by helping him out with the hut chores, as well as helping him with the rainwater collection system, which took her several days to adjust some things and add some others with more innovative ideas. That was the way she showed her gratitude, but her heart wanted to tell him something else that filled her chest with warmth and her belly with passion, with great admiration and respect, and with the desire you feel when the being we love is close to us. As close as when the skin comes to hinder the prisons that insist on looking inside the body passionately an exquisite Mana that will keep them at that moment forever. She loved him.

The insistence of her pimps set her to thinking about how to show him what her heart felt when she saw him arrive because at that moment she felt him close to her, she felt that she was short of breath and became very nervous without knowing what to say or what to do. She did not know whether to stand still or throw herself on top to receive him with a big kiss and take him to bed to make love to him. She had to take on air several times so as not to suffer a cardiac arrest because of the emotion she felt with his mere presence. By that warmth in her chest wanting to escape by her nipples, by the passion in her belly when she saw him in the eyes; for a thousand more reasons that her heart felt.

Many nights she endured to not tell him how she felt and invite him to go up to bed with her, and leave the hammock because she had realized that it was causing discomfort in Philip's back, but Philip did not want to say anything so as not to bother her because he always played strong so that she would not notice. How silly would it be to believe that we deceive them, they realize everything that happens to us; so, she realized his discomfort and wanted him to suffer no more because of her, so she wanted him to sleep in bed with her. Of course, it was because Elida wanted him just like Philip wanted her.

One day she asked him if he wanted to exchange the hammock for the bed for a few days to rest, but Philip did not want to and told her not to worry because he had already gotten used to sleeping in that fishing net-made hammock. She did not insist because she needed it more than he did. Elida did not insist on him knowing he would not change his mind, well there was no way to convince him, he was a confident guy in his decisions. In Philip's heart, there was only the intention to help without taking advantage of under any circumstances; for that reason, she admired and respected him for his firm conviction about the respect of others.

Somehow, in their evening talks, she managed to get closer and closer to him, a little closer at once. With the feminine delicacy that characterizes them when they hit us on the arm, then they hold us with great tenderness to sedate us with their charms, which soften the roughest of men. When rubbing his arm, she lifted his shirt at shoulder height. With delicacy and with great determination she approached him kissing his shoulder tenderly; with the sensual sweetness that characterizes the kiss of a woman in love. Philip felt a shiver from the tip of his feet to the hairs of his head, so he started shaking uncontrollably. He was unable to breathe, but then he felt awake in a way he had never felt before such that at that time he lost all fear and notion of the outside world, being confined in the moment and place as if time did not pass for them. Looking at each other so close as to breathe their breath, which seemed to them a wind with a taste of love. They were lost in the gaze of one in the other, so deeply that they almost came to see internally the soul behind the eyes. They were in love.

They were lost in time and space with a kiss that lasted many minutes, full of much desire felt by both, that they did not mean to stop with their elixir of love. It is there, where we lose the fear of suffering and nothing else matters. Somehow, he had ended up sitting on the bed with her on top of him, as they kissed for the first time.

They made love with the passion of the lovers, letting themselves be carried away with all their desire and without strings attached of any kind, without any modesty or shame. Thus, they consummated the union of their souls and their bodies with all that great passion of youth, but with a maturity full of much knowledge to know how to recognize the good people by seeing them, feeling them, and loving them.

In the morning, they woke up hugging with no intention of getting up to continue the work each took every day. Philip awoke first and brought her something to eat in bed from what had been left over the night before, well they had no time to dine on what he had brought that day. It was obvious that he had preferred to be with her than to eat because love is more important than any need. That new moon Sunday was one of the few days when they did not leave the hut at all.

Elida was nine days away from the end of her menstrual period, being at her most fertile level; besides, she was sure despite the risk. In the same way, Philip did not doubt when assaulted his mind about the possibility of getting her pregnant.

This is the encounter that corroborates the immortality of man granted by God upon the offspring of his blood. As we procreate, we transcend in our personal lesson, and we are leaving behind a little of each one in a new being for a new lesson; that, in time, the universe by divine command will guide some, as well as the last; despite the adversity that this 'Beast of Society' creates to turn us away from the primordial purpose of the spirit, while wandering in time with the living.

By the beginning of spring, they were on their honeymoon on the roof of a small hut that Philip had built in a cave thirty minutes' walk from the dump. In that place they gave themselves to each other in the depths of the gaze, recognizing the love that is seen in the eyes of those who love you, in themselves as they got lost in their gazes.

That bewitching force that pushes us to move forward regardless of adversity or ego, where vanity fades by the fact of gratitude and respect for the common good, that does not demand or seek its own interest, is the one that comes from love.

This magnificent effect of infatuation in Philip made him see that all things possessed a reason that defined them in their form and essence. He realized that his life was getting meaning in a way that he did not expect to happen, but he felt fully prepared to continue discovering that feeling that confuses many in pain and ignorance. Each one must examine yourself before looking for something in others that you think you need.

All that subliminal mystic, which is experimented with love, encouraged Philip to go beyond the dump for the first time in his life. Before nothing had motivated him to leave that place where he had grown up and shared with his parents his better times. Well, it was precisely that what kept him always in the same place, the memory he had and did not want to lose over his family. Over time, that became his comfort zone, which he did not mean to leave for any reason.

Elida brought him new challenges that filled him with the willpower to get out of the dump without the leader noticing. It was the unconditional support from Elida, which motivated him to get out of the incapacity caused by the suffering of losing his parents.

"They are always in my heart," Philip thought.

Being a considerable distance from the dump, he stopped for an instant in a place he had never been before, thinking of all the fears he had left behind. He understood that day that love was stronger than carnal death, or any belief that pretends to explain what happens when we die or what is after death. Philip knew he loved them even though they had died a long time ago, and he knew that the place or the objects did not matter, just the memory that was kept from the moments we must live next to them.

With the insistence that wanting to see Elida, he would come back about noon to bring her something to eat, then go out again to get something for dinner. The smell of her breath made him sigh like a fool by remembering the throbbing of Elida's heart on his chest, the burning heat of her belly of fire. Which made him delirious by wandering among the streets of the nearby village where he ventured to find something to eat so that he could take to his beloved.

It was on that day that he was lost in love, when in one of the streets where he wandered, he came across a construction site where Chendo worked, his godfather and long-life friend. Chendo recognized him immediately when Philip approached to see what was going on because he had found the construction interesting. The style was somewhat innovative and conventional, and it stood out from the other constructions.

Chendo, then he realized that it was him, addressed him:

"Hi, buddy," he said and asked him, "What are you doing here?"

"You already know," answered Philip.

Chendo was surprised to see him because he knew that Philip did not like to go far. That was the first time he had seen Philip out of the dump; for which, he was very happy to see him at the construction site. They had time to talk and joke for a while, as you do with a great friend.

Philip had tried to teach him to read and write on several occasions, but Chendo never showed an interest in learning. Philip no longer insisted on respecting his decision, understanding that he was not interested in learning because he said that it would not bring him any benefit in the misery in which they survived.

Hearing the uproar between jokes and laughter, the foreman of the site suddenly arrived admonishing Chendo to finish the fence he had asked for three days ago, demanding to know what all that noise was and ordering that he better get to work. He asked Philip to leave the place when seeing him all dirty and ill-dressed. Chendo immediately tried to explain to him the reason for his joy, telling him that it was something strange to see Philip out of the dump. That his reason for having ventured was perhaps that he already had a partner; and for that, he made fun of him because he would have to venture further away to seek the livelihood of his new home.

The foreman did not care in the least for Chendo's explanation and asked Philip again to leave, saying that he did not want to see him out there again and not to make his workers waste their time. But Chendo defended him and told the foreman that he could help them with something, run errands or clean up debris on the site. The foreman stayed thinking for a few seconds, wondering if he had misjudged him and thought to give him the opportunity to speak. The foreman asked him to tell him seriously if he wanted to stay to help in what was possible and asked him to go to the store for some sweet loaves and soft drinks, that when he came back then they would talk about it.

They had been working since they arrived that day because of the demands of the construction engineer who asked them to finish before the set date because if they did not finish on time, he would not pay them. This was the reason they stayed to work late and relentlessly some days, to advance a little further and end on the date set by the engineer.

Philip was not quite sure to stay to work for reasons that only he understood at the time. Chendo had talked to him to convince him to go to the store and then they talked about work. But seeing Philip undecided, told him:

"Look godfather, remember that you already have to hustle it," Chendo insisted. "You are no longer alone," Philip, a little hesitantly accepted.

The foreman gave him the money explaining where the little store was, which was closest to the construction site. Philip left immediately thinking of the things he could buy for Elida so that she could smile. Well, he was willing to do anything in order to see her happy.

The foreman recognized the effort of the workers to try to help him as much as they could, sacrificing a break or two to advance a little more in what was possible. Also, they were doing it very well, despite the delay in the fence, for that he let them take a well-deserved rest. Besides, it was already like three in the afternoon, and they had not taken any rest since they arrived that day at six in the morning, as the way they did almost every day due to the demands of the construction engineer to finish earlier than expected.

On his way to the store, Philip felt that look of contempt on the part of the people who misjudged him for his appearance as a dirty and bad beggar, seeing him pass through the street. It was not that he was such a thing, but people labeled him that way because of all those prejudices we acquire in the media about ideas, which are used against our own, but which most ignore. For things that each can judge by your own way, thus condemning him to the misery that picks up other people's trash. They did not allow him to stay in front of their homes; for, as he walked and lost himself in the endless thoughts of things that worried him, he decreased his steps from time to time, pausing a little to meditate within himself about it; but, at the time, people expelled him, telling him to keep walking, that there were no alms for him in that place. Philip decided to continue to not delay in his mission to bring bread and refreshments to the workers of the construction site, regardless of the ignorance of values that people looked him.

Some of his many thoughts were social inequality and the ignorance of many who judge the poor for not having what the role model of society requires. Philip was reasoning about the misunderstanding of the intentions and hypocrisy of those who pretend to be good in their circle, depending on the model that each follows, or intends to follow.

"How is that we dare to judge others, without knowing our own condition?" Philip wondered as he walked.

A couple of blocks from the store he realized the uproar of some children playing marbles on one side of the street. They were arguing because one of them did not want to let a little six-year-old come into the game.

When Philip arrived close to where the children were and not wanting to intervene in the slightest in the matter of the game, he stood across the street to contemplate that scene. Paying great attention to what was going on with the boy, who reminded him of his own childhood when he had to suffer from the imposed by the greedy by taking away what little he found in the trash. He saw himself in that little boy.

The little one said to them,

"I bet all my marbles." Then, one of the biggest kids who always took advantage of everyone faced the little boy very angrily:

"Shut up, fucking gossip. You have nothing," he shouted with imposing fury on his face. "Get out of here, fool." The little one, pulled out his bag of marbles leaving the kid enraged by not knowing what to say. Taking advantage of the moment, the others mocked the oldest, only to further increase his fury. This abusive confronted the little one face-to-face with his fists and wanted to hit him. The little one did not lower his face and stared him in the eye, serenely without saying a word, confident in himself.

The other children started to make a circle defending the little one by saying to let him play because he got marbles. That, what was his excuse now?

A little one of a few three years old, without any fear or issue, with that innocence that characterizes children, said, "Or are you afraid? Chuyito has marbles."

Beginning to encourage others with what he had said, who followed him, shouting all for the little one at the same time:

"Let him play, play, play!"

The biggest boy had no choice but to accept that the little kid played along with two other children who also supported the little one to play. This tall imposing kid felt he could earn some marbles by taking advantage of them, believing they would be easy prey for him.

It was obvious that that was one of their favorite pastimes for all those kids on that street full of bitterness. They had a hole already designated for the game near an almost collapsed adobe wall. The entire play area was free of any stone that would cause them drama or quarrels at the time throwing away their marbles, and it even had a designated area for onlookers. In addition, the line or streak they used to make their shots was defined deep enough that it would not be erased by the rain so easily.

Everyone gathered around the playing area as the players took shooting positions according to what had been imposed on them the biggest boy, who proclaimed the right to throw first trying to take advantage of the others. As he usually does. Besides designating who would throw second and third, left the little one at the last turn. No one claims anything because the boy turned around to challenge them in case anyone opposed his decision. Then, he lined up the players at the shooting line where he thought they would not have a good chance of hitting any marbles. Feeling satisfied and confident, he set out to throw his marbles in the hole.

Trying to throw out as many marbles as he could, the abusive shot with great precision left only about three marbles out of the hole, of ten marbles that each player should throw in his turn. That was a rule more imposed by the oldest boy trying to take advantage of others with his attitude of pride and imposingness.

The second and third were not very precise because of the pressure that the boy exerted on them, failing with a very considerable number of marbles outside the hole, which add to the criticism of the awkward telling them that they lacked the character to face him. The children did not say anything, they just looked at each other. The little kid was in the middle of the shooting line when the oldest one took him off with a blow to the shoulder vigorously.

"Get off, asshole," he told him.

At the very moment when he was throwing his marbles into the hole. Then this abusive guy set out to throw his shot. He aimed and hit a marble.

Hitting one on the first attempt allowed you to keep throwing until hitting as many marbles as possible, for everyone you hit could throw it in the hole. If an opponent's shot was hit by any player, was disqualified from the game. Failure to hit any attempt should be expected to throw again in the order of shooting, starting with the first and so on. Hitting all the shots of the players, you won no matter how many marbles remain.

The haughty kept shooting having hit his first attempt, hitting five more marbles, but when he aimed at his seventh victim, he failed, filling himself with anger because he was near where the little one was standing to whom he growled angrily. The abusive one was blaming him for causing the failure and tried to hit him on the head. But he could not because the little one put up his hands defending himself from the great imposition of the abuser. The other children defended him by claiming that there was still another one to throw, and together they raised their voices supporting the little one, as well as the second and third to try their shots.

The second shot after a big fuss hit four marbles but failed on his fifth attempt, giving the third the possibility of hitting him when he is between the hole and the shooting line. The third aimed as precisely as he could and threw his shot with the intention of hitting the second, being some marbles closer to the shooting line. However, he did not hesitate to try to remove him from the game. By throwing very hard of the anxiety of getting it right, failed and landed right into the hole.

The biggest boy, seeing that the third had drowned, pounced to try to get the second out of the game. The other children intervened by saying that he should let the little one throw because that was his turn in the game, or it was that he was afraid. Which provoked the great anger of the boy by confronting the little one with his fists.

"If you hit me you will see," he told him.

As this abuse had been not far from the shooting line, there was the possibility of being disqualified by the little one. He noticed when the little boy pointed his shot at him, he got very angry, pulling out of his sleeve a new rule, that he could not shoot at him because he was near the shooting line, that he should throw around the area of the hole first, and that if they did not want to do so, he would do something about it to get them to accept. With his fists facing everyone, beating them on his chest, convincing them without any objection, they were all afraid to face him because he was always hitting whoever he wanted just to take away anything he envied of them.

The little one had no choice but to throw close to the hole without being able to hit any marbles because the tyrant prevented him from, aiming at him where he should throw. And he stood in front of the marbles in his way with a high grotesque attitude that no one dared to confront him by fear.

This poorly educated and abusive kid was a very pampered child by his dad from the time he was a baby until he became his own portrait of abusive and haughty with others. He let him do whatever he wanted and gave him everything he asked, despite his mother trying to instill some responsibilities at home, as well as how important mutual respect is, without the child taking it into account on any occasion. Because the machismo that the father instilled in him from a young age, caused him to degrade his mother's posture, in such a way that he yelled at her and beat her up if not for what he wanted at the time. As he had learned by his father's example, to such an extent that the child ended up losing respect for his mother, thanks to the aggression the father gave her and the way he always degraded her. All this led her to become a miserable being with no hope, without any regard from her three children she had with that ignorant monster. Over time they became like him, the same inconsiderate ones who never listened to her in what she advised them to do. They treated their mother like a maid all the time, demanding of her instead of asking her, with the argument their father always told them, that she had no say over them. She took refuge in the only corner of the house where she could find the moment when no one was there to let go of the sea that formed her tears, for all those years of suffering that caused her the indifference of those she loved most in life. Ungrateful.

"Poor creatures who suffer from family cruelty, poor beings who are lost by the evil teachings of others tortured by life, no one ever taught them love," thought Philip when understanding that spoiled child.

Seeing that the little boy's shot was not far away to leave him out of the play, knowing his turn, he pushed a boy who was on his way out of his way hastily to make his shot, with an evil joy while still staring at the little boy's shot. In that, he remembered the second that had been left close to him, and leaned a little forward, taking advantage to hit him harder.

"I got you, dog," he told him, leaving the kid out of the play.

There were only two left. Everyone was silent. Suddenly, one screamed, "If he drowns, he loses!"

The oldest boy turned to look at who had said that, but as everyone was silently attentive to the shot, he turned his gaze to the shot of the little one getting ready to make his shot.

The little boy's shot had landed between him and the hole, so he took a few seconds before throwing a slow and soft shot, enough to hit it without falling into the hole. But, for some strange reason of fate, he could not hit it, and he fell near the hole at the mercy of the little one's shot. Everyone was astonished, including Philip who approached a little mid-street to better see the drama that was happening amid those children of life. "The children of our planet." It was as often Philip referred to them.

The biggest boy got angry in such a way that he clenched his fists with intent to punch the little one in the face but only stared at him almost throwing himself at him. The little boy stood firm in his posture without showing any fear, noticing security in himself that was reflected in the frightened face of the oldest boy. All the children claimed for him, breaking the silence shouted:

"Let him throw, let him throw!"

Without taking his eyes off the little one, he agreed and said, "Well if he drowns, he loses, and I win." The little one settled in to make his shot in a very peculiar way leaning on his left knee forming a right angle with the ground, stretched out his right leg to lean a little better, and aiming at the tyrant set out to mark the history now. They were all silent, and all you heard was the breath of the biggest kid enraged to know he was lost in the game.

The pressure on his finger was adjusted with his gaze fixed on his target without any haste or fear affecting him. Somehow, the kid synchronized himself in every plane of his being to the extent that he was surprised at one point but continued in the scene where his body was. There was a moment when he could see what things are really like, but only for an instant; though, in that instant, he felt as if he were coming out of his body. The little one was about to have an epiphany in his personal fulfillment in such a way that his mind and spirit came together in one goal to defeat the tyrant abuser in front of everyone and once and for all.

With a gentle and accurate stroke, he threw the liar into the hole, leaving his shot in the place where the biggest one was. Then, the arrogant abuser kicked the little one in the face and grabbed with both hands all the marbles he could. The others when they saw what was happening, they jumped on the leftover, passing on top of the little one without caring. After looting, they all ran.

The little one ended up lying on the ground without being able to breathe. When he recovered some strength, stretched out his hand trying to grab some marbles that would have been left over from the looting, but could not rescue a single, one due to the kicks he received from others.

At that moment, he understood everything and forgive his aggressors, while still lying on the ground stretching out his hand, in his aberration to save some marble. Gave up the conflict for an instant as he regained his breath and his body remained in life.

"Who loses and who gains from my suffering?" thought that little being.

Philip, seeing that they assaulted him, lay upon them, so they all run frightened, leaving alone the little kid. These looters will hurt him even more than they left him, without any regard for his property or for his life. Thanks to Philip's intervention they escaped, bluffing their loot among them.

Verum

After a few seconds of Philip approaching to help the child, a bitter whirl that was not coming from the child was heard, but it came from across the street where there was a house built out by the conquerors who crossed those places long ago. The explorers had built a house on top of ancient ruins, but time was tasked with destroying their conspiratorial archetypes for covering up the truth, and only the ruins remained with very little of *the Crusaders* had to do for hiding their trace, as well as their purpose.

The Old Lady with the White Hair, who lived in those ruins, had been the one complaining about what she had seen before her eyes, for like Philip, she witnessed all the drama of marbles and the aberration of man for the least relevant to his spiritual growth.

The Old Lady was at the top of the ruins raising her spear to the sky and shouting, "In what man has become, which only evil inherits!"

Philip ignored her a little for helping the little one but thought somehow that mysterious lady was right, knowing himself how men had contaminated their hearts.

Recalling at the time of his commission, rushed to fulfill the diligence that had been commissioned by the foreman of the construction site, right after he left the little kid in a better mode.

The architecture of the ruins had captured his interest for some mysterious reason that was yet to be discovered, and he kept seeing what he could. But by rushing to the store, he could not look as he would have wanted, staying with the doubt to come back to find out more of that place that he found fascinating.

The Old Lady looked at him from the top of the ruins as he passed back, but Philip, trying to see as much as he could, did not pay much attention to the Old Lady. Seeing her out of the corner of his eye, he thought, "God and his mysteries."

He returned as fast as he could while thinking about what had happened with the children and the mystery that those ruins kept. There was something that made him feel attracted to those ruins in a subliminal way that made him uncomfortable, even though he was willing to find out what it was about.

When they saw him arrive, everyone shouted at him about things, while others blessed him in a very candid way because of how happy they were to see that he brought them something to eat, glad to know that they would finally eat something after many hours of work.

After the concern relaxed with the food, the foreman asked him if he wanted to work with them doing errand jobs or helping the master masons in whatever it took. Philip stood thinking a little first before answering him because he was still thinking about those ruins, and at the same time tried to understand what had happened to the mystery of marbles. Well, he could not pinpoint the lesson of everything that had happened at the time. He would have to live much longer for him to realize the reality of his destiny, as well as the mystery that the ruins kept to him.

"He is just married, my Uicho," Chendo told the foreman. With such rascality, everyone laughed at that moment.

"Precisely," answered the foreman.

Philip thought he would not have the time to see Elida more often and that worried him, besides that he had never worked outside the dump, or anywhere else. He was not accustomed to social responsibilities, nor their foolishness to measure time by naming days by names and hours with numbers. That was all new to him, for so he had a lot to think about before he accepted that he would not see her until he got out of work in the afternoons.

Not wanting to be part of a role model in society, he remained isolated from the philosophy we all take when it comes to wanting to be someone. Although, somehow, he was still part of it without remedying it in any way. That is why he accepted that new challenge in his life, knowing that it would bring new experiences and that he would learn a lot more about what he already knew. Even though he was a little lacking in the practice of many of his knowledge and dexterity skills, he would apply them in an unexpected way.

The foreman told him that he would pick him up in the morning and take him back every day, so he would not worry. In addition, his neighbor would let him know what time they would get out of the dump so he can be ready. He would charge him a penny a week and give him five pesos of salary, which Philip accepted a little surprised because he did not know exactly the value of the money, but he thought that that might bring something to eat every day to his beloved. They usually went out at five in the afternoon every day, but the foreman asked him to stay and help his neighbor with a mixture of stucco, which Philip did the rest of the afternoon. At the end of what he had been assigned, he was quick to leave immediately to see if he could take a closer look at the ruins, but the foreman told him not to leave because he would take him in a while when he finished with a small matter regarding the blueprints of the construction.

"Yes godfather, wait. It is too late for a walk," Chendo told him.

Philip had no choice but to accept the offer that Uicho had humbly asked him when he offer to take him back. Uicho had already told him that he would ride him every day, but Philip had other things on his head that made him forget what he had told him.

He had a very good education that he had learned from his parents in the sufficient time that they were by his side, which is why he accepted. Besides, he knew that he would arrive sooner to see Elida.

Because despite spending his time trying to decipher his fate at every moment of his experiences, thought of her as you think of someone you love, with the passion of the lover and the respect with which one lives near them; with the awareness of the presence of the other, now they share together their time.

"What such of coincidence of fate," Philip said, referring to the luck we have in knowing the others who live in our time.

Chapter 4
Vestiges from the Past

The foreman took them every day after work to the bank of the dump and picked them up in the mornings in the same place on his Apache from nineteen thirty.

"It was a junk beauty," Philip said, when he meant that truck, they called The Zorro.

They had to wind it up with a lever in front of the engine to get it started. It was a daily feat the rite they had formed to perform this task, which they even took shifts when they could not start it so easily.

Two young men worked on the construction site beside his neighbor Chendo, who lived in the dump as well. They recently arrived without anyone noticing how or when. There was a very peculiar young man who they called "the Saint," who was the foreman's nephew supposedly. He had a very cadenced way of speaking, with a peace that relaxed you when you heard him, and sometimes it seems as if he transmitted it to you with his mere presence. The Saint had endless details that Philip found strange and mysterious all the time. Like if there was something else behind that character that intrigued him in such a way that he presented him as a being of peace, of harmonious light that welcomes man in his frequency, in his spiritual harmony. It was because of this feeling that led Philip to engage in a conversation with him on the way back to the dump, for the Saint offered to go with them outside. Well, he had yielded his place in the truck's cockpit to another of the helpers, who was the only one he chatted with more than anyone else.

They introduced each other very cordially, for which even provoked the candid taunts of Chendo and the other assistant, fining them introducing each other. With such a fuss they did not stop laughing when attacking the respectful cadence of their introduction. They ignored them because they were the way life had formed them, well they were the stinging conscience of the divine on the material plane, according to their designs for the good of the spirit of each one.

"Philip," he told him bowing his head. "Please to meet you""-Francesco," said the Saint, bowing back to him, "it is my pleasure.""What do you think of social inequality?" Asked Philip.

Leaving the funny people quiet in anticipation of how he would respond.

"It's disrespectful," the Saint replied.

No muckiness would disapprove of such an answer, nor could argue any pretext that demined the young apprentice of a mason, by the way. Because nobility has no prejudices, and Francesco reflected it in the simplicity of his being harmonized with all his feeling.

His answer was concrete that no one could say anything about it, nor did Philip dare to contribute to the subject because he had deciphered it in a clear and real way.

The Saint was looking inside the truck cockpit as he said his answer. He was watching the other young man inside the cockpit riding with Uicho and the same to whom he had given his place to travel with Philip and the others in the back of the truck. Philip lost his gaze on the horizon imagining the details that that young man should have lived as if to decipher it so concretely and without shoving; besides, it caught his attention on the mystery between that man in the truck's cockpit and Francesco. And so, the amber of the sunset made him travel to the world where our minds are confused by seeking answers to everything.

"What's your story?" Philip asked.

"I studied psychology enough not to want to be a psychologist—for spiritual reasons." He paused and then he said, "Then, in the seminar, I looked for the answer that defined who I am, but I was only long enough not to want to be a preacher. Now, I am here helping and learning about what it is my turn to live. Sharing the moment close to others in the work to continue learning from my destiny and my obligations as a spirit." He responded with his peculiar cadence and fluency in the safety of his words, which he left everyone thinking of their own reasons.

Philip thought that it would be difficult to work without expecting any remuneration because the enjoyment of goods and services requires a bond that represents a value for such. But, to Philip that was normal, so it did not take him much work to understand it because the Saint also mentioned that he did not do it for money, only for the food they could give him.

The Saint mentioned something about the love and the loss of dreams that caused a lump in Philip's throat, as did his neighbor Chendo, well their eyes were so wet that they almost cheered up crying, but they resisted the desire by swallowing their pain by their own reasons that life had taught them.

"Did you fall in love?" Philip asked him. Chendo also asked him at the time.

"How many times did my Saint fall in love?" He stared at him with great tenderness and replied.

"You only fall in love one time in life. If it is not real, then it is not," and confidently continued: "When it happens to you, it will be once and for all." In that, Chendo interrupted him again with a question that intrigued Philip, who turned to see the Saint now.

"What if one dies, my Saint?" He smiled incredulously. "What happens then?"

The Saint, very calm and turning to see Philip in the eyes said: "Love does not die with the body. We do not stop loving those who have died. They have already done their part, and it is quite possible that they will ascend to another plane, but they will never stop loving us, even if we are still alive."

The village lights were lost behind mounds of soil between the village and the dump.

As night fell, they reached the shore where the foreman and the Saint left them and agreed to pick them up early in the morning. "Don't rush sir, see you here," Chendo said, meanwhile the Saint said goodbye to the one who was going in the truck cockpit.

That young man put his hand on the Saint's head and prayed for him, just as the Saint blessed him and put his hand on his chest. They said goodbye to those mysterious young men, as usual, then everyone took their way to their respective huts.

Philip and Chendo's huts were nearby, for they walked together and discussed the details of the work and the obligations Philip had to face in being there. Philip interrupted him by asking him about the other two workers who had walked together to the new hut that was near the old eucalyptus that his grandfather had planted. Philip could see that they were entering that hut that was at the back of the dump.

Chendo realized that Philip did not know about those young men, so he told him that it was a new hut that some Baptist missionaries had made months ago.

"Sure. They appeared after the storm," Philip thought.

After agreeing on the time, they should be ready in the morning to wait for the foreman and the Saint to pick them up to go to work, they said goodbye as they always did since they were kids.

"You settle down, belly," Philip told him jokingly.

"I keep it to you monk," Chendo smiling answered him.

"That is not an offense, fool," Philip said.

"Good night," Chendo said.

"You too, rest," Philip told him, smiling back.

Philip was a little worried about how he would explain to Elida the fact that he could no longer spend time with her, and that she would have to manage some on her own in some things. Perhaps Philip did not value her yet as the independent woman she was, or he cared about her because he loved her, of course, he was in love.

Elida was preparing some dinner for when Philip arrived to eat together, with that feminine intuition that senses things inadvertently because everything was ready the moment Philip arrived. She ran to hug him when she saw him enter and after kissing him passionately said:

"Okay, I miss you a lot. Where were you? And it was time for you to arrive ungrateful."Philip took her in his arms with great joy, staring her in the eye, recognizing love in her gaze and sincerity in her words, then he said:

"I got a job." She jumped on top of him in a leap of joy, kissing him everywhere.

That night, they replaced their evening debates for a serious talk about some issues she knew were important to him, those issues he should face with his philosophy about his concept regarding money, for-profit goods, and services. Perhaps, for fear of his fate he already felt, besides for other things he learned from the way he had been raised. And because she knew him that way, asked him if he was ready to face the challenge that society demands in its model. Philip assured that his soul was not contaminated with ego, but he knew that it would take goods to be able to live worthily if they intended to start a family. Philip told her that he was ready to learn as much as he could in this life to get ahead together.

"You are my Quixote, brave madman," Elida told him, while she was looking at him with great tenderness, that Philip had no choice but to kiss her.

Then they stripped their names and loved each other no matter the tomorrow, or yesterday, just their intimacy as close as possible to each other. The moment every couple knows, where the intent is introduced into the temple of fire, even the bodies seem to get in the way when trying to touch their souls.

At five in the morning, Elida prepared him six bean tacos with pepper and mango water in an old cantina, which she had to fix some slats so Philip could hang on his shoulder. Philip hung it proud of it, for she had made something that he had planned to do for a long time ago. Philip kept it in the trunk that his father inherited from him, in which Elida had found Philip's mother's diary. So it was, as he realized that she had opened the trunk, but said nothing, he was silent thinking that the time had come to open his complexes, taking them out of the trunk, so that they do not impede the advancement of the spirit and the learning in this life.

He said goodbye to her with a kiss, but she prolonged it for a couple more minutes before letting him go.

"Walk my Quixote," Elida told him, "Go confidently now. I can't wait for you to tell me how you did it."

Philip stopped before leaving to see her one more time.

After kissing her one more time with the intention of never leaving, he left to meet Chendo at the edge of the dump, to chat a little bit before the foreman arrives. Those two mysterious young men were already waiting for them to arrive.

"Good day," Philip and Chendo said at the same time.

"Are good days," one of them said, the other one just nodded his head.

At that moment, the foreman arrived shouting from afar in the form of a slather, and very happy everyone, almost running, climbed The Zorro. The Saint was not with Uicho that day, so Chendo took advantage and went with the foreman in the truck's cockpit, the other two went with Philip in the back of the truck.

They did not mention any words most of the way until they arrived near the village where the construction site was. Philip was stretching out his head trying to see something of the house where the Old Lady lived, though he was more interested in the architectural design with which the ruins underneath had been built. He felt somewhat anxious at the time, waiting for the opportunity to go to investigate a little more about the mystery of The Old Lady with the White Hair, and that masterwork that had been done by a lost civilization. Time took care to resurface what was buried under that old house made by the Jesuits, as they passed by on their way protecting and caring for the holy objects, touched by the divine.

"One feels it. Right?" one of the deputies said, as Philip stretched out his head, for his spirit called him to his destiny.

Philip said nothing when he heard what that beggar had said because he was trying to see the ruins that had captivated him with great interest, but he thought about it and tried to ask the young man something about it. For some strange reason he could not tell him anything, he could only look him in the eye for a moment because there was something very strong about that young man that Philip felt in him and because he did not feel privileged to be able to speak to him, he could not say a single word. He did not know why, but that is what Philip felt.

The foreman delegated the obligations as he always did every day so that each one would take care of their part, so they would try to build as much as they could. The engineer had repeatedly threatened Uicho that he would not pay him a penny if he do not finish on the time he has already set. He state to him clearly who was the boss, then warned him that they better hasten to finish as soon as possible and that he wanted no objection; because if so, he would fire him along with his beggars. That is how the engineer told Uicho that day as he went through the construction site. The engineer was along with three other individuals who were taking data of what he told them as he showed them the site.

At the end of the tour was that the engineer talked to the foreman.

"Yes engineer, as you say. Okay, I will do it, you will see," Uicho answered to everything the engineer was telling him.

The engineer turned around whispering something that left Uicho thinking about all those years he had worked for him: "Ignorant."

Uicho listened to him but said nothing because he felt he had a responsibility to fulfill with his work boys, who were always faithful to him. He had a responsibility to his family, above all. What could he do? he had seven children to support.

"You must, my Uicho," the engineer told him, the moment he got in his car to leave with his friends.

Uicho just nodded and went to rush the workers a little more than usual, and even some were surprised to see him serious as if some energies of the engineer were still in him. Uicho was a very cheerful and accommodating person in his work, who always liked to joke with everyone. He promoted joy to overlap the dissatisfaction with some duties because he believed that if joy exceeded the dissatisfaction with obligations, everything could be made easier and faster. So, he was always trying to set an example with a willingness to do things, enjoying the time of the task, and showing the example of dedication with his effort in everything he did, which conveyed a good vibe to his companions with his joy.

Despite being in charge of the construction site, he was always a good worker because he always worked hard in everything he did. The simple nobility of his way of being represented him as a great example for many, especially to those he had taught to work as crafts-men in construction.

Due to the rush over the foreman's neck was that they took the break time until three o'clock in the afternoon, well they were so tired and hungry that he felt sorry for them. He told them that they could take a break to eat something, for he was working forced marches too, with the same tiredness and hunger they felt. When they saw him in a hurry, they supported him without saying anything but working at the same pace as him.

"So much for so little," Uicho said. The young man who accom-panied him in the truck's cockpit back to the dump the day before was close at the time, and he approached by touching Uicho's shoul-der recognizing his inner goodness. The young man smiled at him very pleased to see that his intentions were good.

"Go to lunch, it is too late," said Uicho. The young man turned around taking the other three who were working along with them.

"Come on, come on boys, let us go for something to eat," he said with a very peculiar charisma in his person that caused the foreman's smile.

Some workers who lived in that village gathered to eat as they did every day to share their food. Philip noticed when the other young man who lived in the dump interrupted them by asking them if he could bless the food first; for which they willingly accepted. Chendo told Philip that they always ate together with the others since they arrived at the construction site. Also, they always talked about strange things that he did not care about, well he always had to work to bring something to eat to his family and did not have time for that nonsense.

Philip could see the foreman and the Saint sharing their meals while talking about some personal issues. He felt something strange in his belly, as if he wanted to go ask him something, but he didn't know what it was that he wanted to ask him. He felt an internal conflict immediately as if there was something that attracted him and drove him away from that young Saint that could not come clear to his mind. The truth was that he wanted to go see the ruins and investigate the mystery he felt had brought him to where he was.

"Where do you go, Monk?" Chendo asked him.

"It is said, fool. Fool," Philip said, almost about to walk the way to that place. "The shopkeeper owes me a pop for helping him with a few lumps."Philip ran away to the ruins to find out more about his fate that deliberately left its hints in his dreams. Because they were very good friends since they were children, they made fun of each other in everything they did; also, they relied on any rush, to such an extent that Philip came to love him as a brother.

Arriving at the corner where that place was located, Philip realized that the remnants of the original ruins spanned the entire block because it was full of bulges of buildings buried by time. At least it was that what Philip intuit as he contemplated such a great work. He thought those men must have made a great effort in their work, having built such a place. He was sure that there were more buildings beneath those mounds of earth.

There were houses that people had built around the main part near these mounds of earth that stood out around the construction site. Some built their houses on top of these mounds without knowing what was under their feet.

That is how he realized that the house had been built on top of one of these mounds of earth, but as he approached, he discovered signs of deterioration from the rain and the time that leave nothing hidden. He was able to see architectural vestiges of an ancient construction under the mound, where the house had been erected by the conquerors.

He arrived at the entrance of the house with his heart rate a little high, due to some design that fate had already announced to him in one of his dreams because Philip already presented in some way what was about to happen.

The Old Lady was sitting on top of a blue stone that was in the middle of the hall of the house deteriorated for centuries. Trying to keep fear away, Philip entered cautiously to where the Old Lady was.

"I was waiting for you," said The Old Lady with the Woolly Hair.

He felt that he could not breathe when he saw the Old Lady not move her lips when saying that when he had heard her perfectly inside his head.

"How is that possible?" Philip asked her.

"Sit down," the Old Lady told him.

He felt a little more confident to see that it was her lips that pronounced those words, somehow, he had learned to differentiate between when he listened with his ears and what he had heard inside his head. Philip was too sane to fancy, though he did not close himself to any possibility, and on this occasion, he would not waste the opportunity.

"Who built the ruins?" Philip asked as he sat in front of her.

"There were other men before you who also had dreams but succumbed to their fears," the Old Lady told him.

Philip did not understand very well what the Old Lady was saying to him because for him there was no sense in fears and dreams. Although, he sensed a little because, somehow, he imagined what might possibly have happened with these men, considering what was going on at the time everywhere in the world, and he found a great similarity to those who had lived before.

The Old Lady had mentioned the idea indirectly, but Philip intuited very well by approaching his judgment, comparing our fears with the fears that made us succumb to the dreams of those who lived before all of us.

Philip had read history but did not remember seeing this part about dreams lost by fear, the subject was something new to him. He focused his attention on everything the Old Lady told him about the history of the original people that had built that city forgotten by men, of everything that had to happen. Waiting for a sign that gives him a reason why those men had lost their dreams, those who had likewise tried it just as we do today, Philip had no choice but to concentrate on what she told him.

The Old Lady with the Woolly Hair told him that already being ruins that place, was discovered by the Jesuits who built a temple on top of those ruins, trying to hide them in some way, for reasons that he was yet to discover.

"What were they hiding? What is this place really?" asked Philip. She just looked at him and smiled a little.

"The truth is much bigger than anything in your life. If you want to know more, you must be patient," the Old Lady told him.

Philip kept thinking a little about everything the Old Lady had told him, but he remembered that he should return to work on the construction site, for he stood up immediately and walked quickly towards the entrance. She stopped him telling him:

"Everything has a beginning; this is the time for you to begin your journey to the truth. Come on," she beckoned him with her hand.

Philip approached immediately almost without thinking of it and knelt in front of her.

"Put your hands on your chest," the Old Lady requested.

Then she put the spear on Philip's shoulder, saying, "

If you are to look for it, you must still commit to protecting it."Philip raised his head and answered her:

"I will do it."She slapped him with her left hand.

"So, you would not forget it," the Old Lady told him.

Philip rose rubbing his jaw looking at the Old Lady sideways and left almost running back to the construction site, for he had felt that it had been a long time, and he was worried about being scolded for being late to work.

He had not obtained the answers he wanted, and he had left with more unknowns than with those he had come with, for all that the Old Lady had initiated him with the task of protecting the truth. His concept and perception of reality, as well as his upbringing, did not allow him to fully accept what had happened, but he knew he was not crazy, he had not imagined all that.

Returning to the construction site he found the foreman and the Saint watching closely the blueprint.

He approached them a little without asking anything, as Chendo approached also to see what was going on.

The blueprint had the design of an entrance with nine pillars on each side, with a length of twenty-seven meters, a height of three point three meters, and three-point-fifteen meters wide. With a house covering all vestiges of ruins around. There were three mounds of earth in the middle of where the house was supposed to be built. One of six meters high, and the other two of four meters high. The engineer had ordered the mounds of earth to be removed to carry out his work, but when they dug, they found that they were very old architectural constructions, and what was sticking out of the ground was just the tip of those constructions.

The Saint sensed that Philip was approaching from behind them and turned to see him at the time. Philip bowed to him with his head, as the Saint reached out to call him to come closer.

Philip had all kinds of knowledge thanks to the books his father had inherited him, in addition to those found in the trash, and for all that, his mother had taught him. Reading blueprints was one of that knowledge that almost no one knew he had, except for Elida and his neighbor Chendo, who were the closest to know him. They knew about his great talent to serve and help without expecting something in return, of his skill to fix all kinds of gadgets and strange things that almost all ignore how they work. He was a Jack of all trades who enjoyed helping everyone.

The foreman did not object to the Saint inviting Philip to see the blueprint, even without knowing that he could read it very well, he was silent, stepping aside so Philip could see it better.

Philip realized that the values of the arch dimensions did not match the dimensions of the width of the pillars that would sustain it and that the house would remain above the ruins they had unearthed, which would be a sacrilege such a scoundrel. Philip knew that the engineer had told them to remove all those stones because Chendo told him that he had listened to the engineer tell the foreman about it that day that he had gone through the construction site.

Philip realized that the blueprint had been integrated into three distinct phases, highlighting the style of each of the designs in each phase. In addition, the dimensions of each phase had not been adequately integrated between them. There were sections in all phases that had been erased, not very successfully because you could see the lines a little bit.

The design of the central part of the house, which averages six meters high by fifteen wide and fifteen meters long, was above the tip coming out of the pyramid. It had two habitations on each side three meters high, six meters long, by six meters wide, with a small room in the back of the central gallery. The entrance with the pillars had been designed straight, regardless of the slope of the small hill where they intended to build it.

"Now, he even reads blueprints," said the foreman.

"I told you he was weird, body," answered Chendo, meanwhile the Saint just laughed a little, and asked Philip if there was anything else on the blueprint that was wrong, or misplaced.

"It seems as if different people designed this blueprint, my Saint," Philip replied.

The foreman took the blueprint to see for himself, asking Philip to show him the details where he believed there were mistakes. He was not convinced of that beggar's experience, but he was right, and the foreman knew it from his own experience, only that Philip had noticed more mistakes than he had seen, so he agreed with Philip in all the details in which there were dimensional errors. He stared at Philip in amazement as he suggested ideas to integrate everything into a much better and more practical design, with only a few adjustments to the blueprint, along with what they had built up to that point.

The foreman, recalling the engineer's threats, found himself between the sword and the wall without knowing what to do at the time, was only very dismayed with his hands on the blueprint that was spread over the table.

The Saint took him by the shoulder very gently and said: "It is time to face your fears."Philip felt his heart want to get out of his chest when he heard the Saint say that. An avalanche of thoughts invaded him now, which connected with The Old Lady with the White Hair.

"Go to work back there Chendo," said Uicho very seriously.

"Go with him," the Saint asked Philip who, understanding the situation, went with Chendo to continue working on a part that seemed to have no problem.

The engineer was very clear in his threats when he told Uicho that he wanted no more pretexts or delays regarding the work and that if he did not fulfill his mandates, he would fire him without re-hiring him for any of his projects. He had given him a month's deadline for the entrance and the front of the house to finish, no more, no less. That was the only thing that came to the foreman's mind at the time when the Saint was trying to bring him into balance. The engineer's claims and threats caused him a nervous breakdown for not know what to do. Standing still thinking for a while about what to do to warn the engineer about the problem they had detected in the blueprint, the entrance, and the slope; as well as the failure to integrate the arch with the pillars.

The foreman had worked with the engineer for many years on many projects and always fulfilled him on time in the deliveries of the works. On his part, the engineer had no pretext to complain about the careful and honest work Uicho always lent with his team of assistants, who always supported him.

The engineer always threatened him to finish on the date he wanted because otherwise, he would not pay him for his work. Being little more than a pittance, what he gave them for what the craftsmen did.

Knowing that he had a family of many children to support, the engineer used to blackmail him by telling him, "Think about the family, Uicho, think about the family."

This left him with no choice but to accept what the engineer demanded of him.

All those years of abuse and humiliation that degraded his person to a simple servant, without any right or respect for the humble work he did, building the homes of the rich and powerful, caused him stressful anxiety that he could not sleep at times at night. He felt that he could no longer resist the stalker's ruthless cruelty, and he was looking for a way to get rid of all that.

"God, give me strength," thought Uicho in those moments of insomnia.

An hour after confronting his fears, he decided to go and call the engineer to warn him of what they had discovered. He taught that the engineer should understand it better than he does and could tell him what to do about it. For that, he would have to go to the post office that was in the village where he lived to be able to call him because that was the only place in the municipality that had a phone.

Having thought very carefully of everything involved in speaking to the engineer to inform him what was going on with the blueprint, decided to take the bull by the horns stopping the whole work at that time. He told everyone that they could leave; to which they all reacted by celebrating very happy, by collecting their work tools to store them quickly so that they could leave as soon as possible. Philip and Chendo took their things to get up on the Zorro. Except for the Saint and one of the young men who lived in the dump.

"What about them?" asked Philip Chendo.

"Only God knows. Let us go, hurry up," Chendo said. "Let us go, we do not have this every day." Philip climbed The Zorro with one more mystery in his busy mind that he did not ask him anymore about, for being thinking about the blueprint, and how to integrate everything into a single design style because that was a challenge that he was excited to take. He imagined designing his own house in his own way, and he thought of making a new blueprint with a different design for the entrance and the facade of the construction.

Because of the foreman's haste for going to tell the engineer, they got to the dump sooner than usual. They almost had to jump off The Zorro to get down as soon as possible.

"Hurry up, quick. I'll see you tomorrow," the foreman told them.

Then he left quickly, leaving Philip, Chendo, and the other young man who lived in the dump amid a cloud of dust, so they had to walk fast to get out of the dust and smoke left by the truck.

"Have a good afternoon," the other young man said, who Immediately went to his hut.

"Same for you," Chendo told him.

"You take care of yourself," Philip told him.

On the way to their huts, Philip did not stand the urge to ask him about the Saint and the other young man.

"You know how the religious are, with their cults and stuff," Chendo said. "Why?"

"I've felt some weird things," Philip said seriously.

"You and your feelings as usual. I am going to take the kids to see if we can see, even a rat, to take advantage of before the night falls. You better go do something to the hut and stop thinking what others do." Philip looked at him for an instant thinking how right that dear friend was.

"You're progressing big cheeks. Who would say about you, that you're pretty funny," said Philip.

"I see you when I get back, fool," Chendo said, leaving towards his hut very excited to see what the children would say.

It was so long a time since they had hunted because he was always working on the construction site that the children were glad when they saw that he had arrived early at the hut and sensed that he would tell them that they would go hunting for the rest of the afternoon. Philip could hear the joy of the little ones as they saw their father come home and that they would spend some time with him.

An endless of emotions invaded his chest, remembering when his father returned from his day and took him hunting in the evenings, which almost nearly cried. He calmed his emotion with a great sigh and rushed to his hut to see his beloved; besides, he had a personal mission to fulfill with that blueprint. He was excited by the idea that he could practice his design skills, knowing that it could be a great challenge for him, which he would not waste; for that, he thought to spend the rest of the afternoon doing his great masterpiece. After all, who keep him from dreaming?

Arriving at the hut, Philip found Elida and two of her cronies fixing a kind of skylight on the roof, amid a big scandal, the same way it is done among great friends. It was clear that they were very well organized because one held the container that Elida used to climb while the other lady passed her a hammer to nail a board that held the plastic mica they had found in the trash.

"Well don't you listen well, that I have told you that a nail beside the hammer? And you do not do that thing of yours to be rocking it, that you are going to make me smash my hand. Then, how do you want me to attend to my male? Fools," Elida told them.

The three cackled for what she had said, at the time Philip entered the hut.

"Virgin of the Candelaria. How is it that you have arrived early, poet? I told you fools but you are reluctant mules like my grandfather's," Elida told them.

She stayed motionless for an instant because at that moment she could remember something from her past without saying anything and a little bewildered that everyone realized.

Philip helped her to get her down from the container where she was standing, asking if she was okay.

"I have remembered something.""Tell me, sweetheart, what is it?" Philip asked her, touching her face with his hands.

Meanwhile, her other two pimps said goodbye to them with some rascality saying that they better leave them alone because of being just married. This is what those pimps called them, when they saw them together, they had just married.

The truth is that they were always her protectors and understood much more than Philip about some things that happened to her.

"To cease to be bad third then," Carmela said, taking Inés with her, who sighed to see them hugged as she walked out of the hut so that even Carmela had to pull her a little so that she would hurry. "Hurry up, fool," she told her, while they were going out.

Inés just screamed a little without so much fuss, rather with some rascality and exaggeration, typical of great friends.

"I'm not sure," Elida told Philip, a little confused, while Philip insisted that she should trust him. "Okay, I'm very sane, you are going to tell me how you have gone? You must have a good of things, my Quixote."Philip had no choice but to respect her silence about what she had remembered, letting her make the decision at the right time to tell him that part of her life that Philip was unaware of.

From start to finish, Philip told Elida about what had happened to him at work, about the problems of the blueprint and things that others did, the mystery that was suspected by intuition, that made him feel a hint of what fate played with its hints. Elida listened to him carefully, only sometimes interrupting him with complements to the ideas that Philip seemed to understand, regarding what was happening in the world daily and how it impacted the spirit of individuals.

"What do you think is the truth?" Philip asked her suddenly, while she was serving some water listening to what he was saying, besides she was trying to clarify in her mind what she had remembered, at the time Philip asked her.

"The truth, I don't know," Elida told him. "But love looks a lot like it."Elida had recalled many things from her childhood, from her parents and grandparents who had taught her that part of the truth is open to all of us, but that we are all mistaken for aberrations for misunderstandings.

The rest of the afternoon, Philip was tasked with making a new design for the entrance and facade of the construction. He had to discuss it with her first, but Elida did not refuse or doubt that he had what is necessary to do it, for she knew him that talent of doing endless weird things; so, supporting him in his enthusiasm, Elida put a small table that she had made just under the skylight that she and her cronies had invented that day, along with paper and a pencil. She opened the windows, which were just a few holes in the hut's walls. She put something to drink nearby and lay down in the hammock to see him all afternoon working on the design he dreamed of would one day be built. The truth is, who would accept his project? if he was an uprooted beggar. Philip knew that the engineer of the construction site would never allow his design to be replaced. Anyway, he did it with great enthusiasm and dexterity like any professional in the field, convinced that he was able to carry out such a task.

"Your grace captivates me," Elida told him, as the sunset was on her back through one of the hut's holes, appreciating the amber of the sunset.

He stopped at times to write something in his little notepad that he always carried with him, where he wrote his thoughts on what he was discovering every day, poetry, and little fables that he suddenly invented in his spare time.

"I love you, my poet. As crazy as the Quixote, that walker of a thousand surprises," Elida told him, as he worked on his dream, then she blew him a kiss with her hand.

"You are my muse, my love" Philip replied.

Then Philip turned his attention to what he was doing because it was important to him, he could not waste much time.

Elida had fallen asleep in the hammock waiting for him to finish. She woke up at five in the morning, which was the time he had asked her to wake him up to get ready to go to work, in case he fell asleep. He always gets up at that time of the morning, but that night he stayed too late trying to finish his design and fell asleep on the table.

She had that well-favored female intuition, which she rushed to wake him up fearing that Philip would not have finished the blueprint, after so much effort and enthusiasm that he had put into it. She went and moved him a little by the shoulder and he awoke right away, a little confused but got up very happy for finishing his dream.

"I got it, skinny!" Philip told her.

"Holy Virgin of the Candelaria!" exclaimed Elida with great relief, that even Philip asked her if she was ok, but she said it was nothing, that she better hurry to prepare him something to eat so that he would not be late to go to work.

Six bean tacos with jalapeño chili were what she fixed him for lunch, with some water in his cantina. Philip thought it was a delicacy. After thanking Elida with a big kiss, he took the blueprint and keep it in his backpack along with the food. Then went to see Chendo and the other two young men wait for the foreman and the Saint to pick them up on the bank of the dump.

The foreman arrived very quiet and thoughtful. The Saint did not come with him, nor did the other young man who lived in the dump come out that day. Nor Chendo, nor Philip dared to ask the other young man about his companion, either wanted to interrupt the foreman to ask him about the Saint, they only climbed The Zorro very seriously when they saw the face of the worried foreman. As Chendo knew him very well, he was surprised to see him so thoughtful and quiet.

Philip found the foreman's silence strange, making him think of what the engineer might have said about the blueprint and its poor integration. He embraced his bag by feeling something, fearing that his work would be in vain, and felt an annoying feeling inside his belly, bittering his hopes of recognition for his skills. He did not say a word all the way, not even Chendo who was more joking than simple, said a single word. Neither the other young man, well at times it felt as if he were not even there as if he only observed without intervening, at least only as necessary. Philip realized the almost sublime presence of those young strangers, but he did not comment on anything with anyone, for he felt that no one would consider his speculations about what was really going on around all; for that, he kept the mystery, to be sure of what he believed before telling anyone else. Even to Elida, he did not tell her a few things.

Many lose credibility with society by touching on issues that are not relevant to people's intimate interests, which are already rooted in the system of life in this modern society, at all economic or cultural levels. Those who enlighten or are free from the system are those who transcend the most in personal truth, those who sacrifice vanity for freedom; those who break the bonds that enslave every man's dream into this modern model.

Upon arriving at the work, the foreman asked them to go to work on the facade of the house, with a serious face without conviction in what he said. He was not looking good because he was very nervous and worried, that he sent everyone to places where they did not usually work. Everyone, seeing him as he was, said nothing, and set out to work. There were whispers among some of them, but he did not take them into account because he was thinking about what the engineer had to tell him, after yesterday he communicated the problems with the blueprint.

The foreman had to return to his village the day before in order to call the engineer, which he tried to do all afternoon without any fortune because the engineer was in a meeting with the Architect. This guy answer him almost at dusk, only to shout to him that he was an asshole, that he let himself be manipulated by an ignorant. That this was the last time he warned him, and that he would go to the construction site to talk to him in person.

That is why he was distraught, he was afraid of losing his job along with that of others, those who always helped him for many years, who had already taken a great affection for how good a person he always was with them. Uicho in turn appreciated them in a great way, and always saw them as friends and companions, rather than as a boss. And he always showed them by the example he set when working very cheerfully and with dedication. He thought of his family first then everything else, on what would happen if he lost his job. Well, there were many children he had, and he could not afford to be out of work. Uicho knew from his experience that something was not quite right with the blueprint, but he had no arguments against the engineer that would give him credibility; at least, he did not have the courage to confront him alone with Philip's tale and his ability to read the blueprint. Ended up almost to the point of a nervous breakdown without knowing what to do. Philip was a little disappointed that the foreman did not tell him anything about the blueprint, for he only saw him when he asked him to help Chendo on the facade, and he did not dare to ask him, he just went straight away to do his duty.

Philip thought endlessly of possible things while working with Chendo on some stones to be placed on the facade of the central building, as directed by the foreman. What else could he do? Take his place and meet the requirements that responsibility requires. Sometimes he would lose self-esteem by thinking absurd things about himself, nor believing himself capable of doing something that could be recognized or admired.

It was like that as he visualized it on some occasions when thought led him back to the vices of the indifferent world; of which he complained about its lack of wisdom, making him fail without thinking about what he was trying to point out in others. Chendo had to interrupt him with more mortar because he was thinking half-stunned, almost talking about what he thought with the grimaces he did.

"Hurry up, the engineer is here, fool," Chendo told Philip, at the time the engineer got out of his car, along with three other guys who followed him to where Uicho was.

From where they were you could hear everything the engineer was shouting at Uicho with a very exaggerated tone. Uicho just closed his eyes and squeezed his mouth, took his hands, and rubbed them in his belly just above his belly button, without being able to say anything. The engineer reminded him that if he did not do what he said he could leave when he wanted and that he would not pay him a penny for what he had already done, he even threatened to hit him if he did not finish the work, in the time he had set him previously.

"Yes sir, as you say," Uicho told him.

The engineer shoved him into one of the back rooms of the main building, which Uicho used as his office, in which he was only seen at the beginning of the workday and at the end of the day because he was always outside working with the others. The room was used to save the work tools, along with the blueprint and other things.

After a few minutes, the screams gave way to a silence that intrigued Philip in a way, that he began to hallucinate related to what was going on inside the room, seeing and hearing everything that was going on in small flashes inside his head. He began to convulse as the visions passed on, for when he closed his eyes the flashes were coming to mind when he opened them woke up.

Chendo, immediately took him by the shoulders talking to him and moving him a little to react. He was a little scared when he saw his eyes roll backward. Philip came back for an instant as he opened his eyes and tried to tell him something. He could not say any sane words and got lost in the vision again by closing his eyes and starting to say what the foreman and the engineer were talking about. Chendo let him go right away and poured a little water on his head to see if he reacted, but Philip continued to speak what they said, almost emulating the tone of voice of each one; so, Chendo was very frightened, that he pushed him a little stronger to react. Then, Philip opened his eyes again.

"What is it? What is the matter with you? Come back, come back Philip," Chendo told him, agitated by the scare.

"Uicho paid everyone with his money," Philip told him very serenely, trying to understand what had happened, not because of his visions, but of what happened to the foreman and the engineer.

Because, according to what he saw and heard, the engineer owed Uicho two months of work, which Uicho had to pay from his pocket to the workers, without them knowing. Because Uicho always showed a good face with them, well every day was the same without showing any problems; for, he was always shown with the optimism that characterized him.

"He faced him," Philip told him looking him in the eye.

Chendo smiled and felt a little better because being his best friend he knew him very well about the sudden attacks that happened to him since he was a child, and when he saw him calmer the scare passed.

Somewhere Uicho had drawn the necessary forces to confront the engineer once and for all, without mind what could happen to him. He interrupted the engineer while he was yelling at him that they would have to finish in the time he had told him because his skin was at stake. Uicho asked him to pay him what he owed him until then, that he would no longer work if that were how he wanted. The engineer was silent for a few seconds to hear him so sure of himself; for, he always folded himself in accordance with everything he demanded, and when he saw his reaction, he did not know what to say.

From one moment to the next the countenance of the engineer changed from offending him to praising him for helping him for so long. Trying to convince him to finish the job in the time he was demanding of him.

"If you want me to finish it, pay me everything at once," Uicho told him with a serious and firm stance, that the engineer swallowed saliva without having anything to say for a few seconds.

"Let us see, let us see, my Uicho. Here are your two months, and if you finish in three months, I will give you two months in advance and the rest when it is done," the engineer told him, with a very persuasive attitude that he denoted that something else was behind all this.

As the engineer got in the car, Uicho arrived at Chendo and Philip, very serious, without the smile he always had.

"Leave that thing alone and go eat," Uicho told them.

"Hell yeah!" They shouted to some who were close to hearing it, and very cheerful left immediately.

Chendo and Philip stayed with Uicho for a few minutes trying to comfort him. He told them not to worry because he knew what he was doing and that they would finish the work just as the engineer had planned.

"Remember the thing that says this fool my Uicho," Chendo told Uicho.

Uicho stared Philip in the eye and told him that he could do nothing because at the end of the day the engineer was the boss, besides he had already paid to finish as it was on the blueprint, within three months.

Philip only nodded his head, took his bag said goodbye to Chendo, and left immediately heading towards the house of The Old Lady with the White Hair in search of answers.

Chapter 5
The Key and the Lost Paradise

Upon reaching the pyramid, the Old Lady waited for him sitting in front of the altar as she always did whenever Philip had time to visit her.

Philip entered the altar without realizing that she was sitting on the bluestone, which seemed to have a light inside that changed between an intense violet to a very translucent blue. Suddenly, the Old Lady moved her spear enough for Philip to realize the movement she had made, being able to see her clearly sitting on the stone. He sat in front of her as she pointed the spear at him.

The Old Lady with the White Hair wore a strange robe that looked as if it was translucent in the wind, making Philip feel a little weird.

"What is it?" Asked Philip, referring to the blue stone.

"You don't eat green figs; you don't cut wheat early," the Old Lady replied.

Philip stood thinking, trying to understand what she had told him, and he thought he should wait for things to come to him differently, instead of asking for answers from someone else. Well, no one will teach you what your thought is like, nor how you must face the challenges that life puts you on the path. It is you who has access to the universe inside, which keeps the knowledge of everything that interferes with the reason for each other's existence.

Although he understood what the Old Lady said, he had concerns about who had built the pyramid and for what purpose, he wanted to know what had happened to them. He felt a shiver as he thought of all those dreams shattered by time, that it did not care how big their effort had been, or the dedication with which they are striving for their lives, well it always changes everything.

In that, Philip noticed a white light intensifying more and more coming out of the Old Lady's head. He felt an electrostatic discharge around that made him feel a little exorbitant, while the Old Lady stared him in the eye.

Philip heard the Old Lady laughing inside his head, for he was a little frightened. He wondered if he was crazy imagining all that, or what was really happening because he had never met someone like her, nor had he seen any stone radiate any light like the one she sat, less listen to someone else's thoughts.

The Old Lady with the White Hair pointed the spear at him right on the forehead and Philip began to have visions of three white pyramids with silver tips, which radiated great energy around the world. There were people and animals who lived in a large city full of gardens and palaces with figures on their facades, representing the path that the spirit takes in carnal life.

They had discovered great power within themselves, but many used it for evil and did not measure the consequences by losing control of what they consumed, desiring more power to dominate the world instead of helping it. Besides, they kept the key to inner wisdom so that the truth would not be known. Giving the privilege to a malicious circle that used wisdom to control everyone's attention, and that is the same control of misinformation that exists in this age.

He could see with the clarity of his mind an intense light on the horizon that spread throughout the planet, then a great flood covering all the cities, killing millions of living beings instantly. Very few places were left untouched by the light and the avalanche of destruction, and some surviving beings took refuge in those places with nothing but their own souls.

Philip looked at the place that had not been touched by the destruction, a man with a gold pectoral and a book in his right hand, another had a crown with precious stones, one with a spear, and one with a medallion on his neck. Among other things, he could not recognize.

Philip immediately recognized the spear, which was the same one the Old Lady had, besides the medallion that the old Suzeo had on his neck.

The Old Lady with the White Hair removed the spear from Philip's forehead, and he opened his eyes for an instant. Then, Philip kneeled with his hands touching his belly because he felt great pain after waking up.

"Who could form the words that describe what you just saw with your own being?"

"No one," Philip answered disappointed.

Philip cried intensely as he remembers the painful faces of those beings who had lost their lives in that divine plan, that had ended the dreams of many innocents, by the guilt of the sloppy insolence of reason for the common good. They lost their hopes because of the senselessness of their petty leaders, who always sought to distract them rather than to attend to them in their inner opening. They gave them the forbidden fruit by abusing their susceptibility. For these like stray sheep ate the wheat leaving the weeds to spread everywhere, polluting the land that fed them, the rivers and seas that gave them to drink. The worse of all, the undergrowth grew so much that reached everyone's heart with pride and great egotism, by the great power they had attained in their technology and wisdom over the universe.

Philip could bear neither the pain nor the anguish in his womb for the loss of those poor souls because he did not approve in his spirit such atrocity against the divine creation, of those beings who built their wrong ideas with the intentions of the highest; and this, deciding for that, extinguish any trace of their foolishness. "God can't be so cruel," Philip said bathed in tears.

He stood up as he could wiping tears with his dirty battered rags, whining, trying to get some air, for the feeling had encumbered his heart in a way, that he kept crying thinking that this might happen to those he loves. The Old Lady put her hand on his chest, making Philip recover some sanity. Within his thoughts understood the revelation, as if somehow, inside of him was reflected the response that the divine took against the foolishness of the foolish indifferent to the common good; but, just for an instant because then he lost the idea at sea of thought.

"Take good care of what your heart desires. You are capable like any other man," the Old Lady told him, while Philip was walking away to go back to work, for he suddenly remembered that he should return because perhaps it was a little late.

He wanted to find out what had happened with respect to the blueprint and the irregularities of integration with the terrain where such a design was intended to be built.

Wanting to return as soon as possible to work, the sea of thought made him forget some details that would be important in his personal lesson. The peculiarity of the moment covered him with more questions in his mind, not knowing what his spirit really needed to transcend the ideal he espoused with his philosophy of life.

Upon returning, he found the foreman standing in front of the main building, which was where it would supposedly end the entrance with the pillars.

Not knowing what to do, Uicho was just standing there watching the slope where the pillars for the entrance would be built, trying to figure out how to accommodate it as best he could so it would not collapse.

Philip approached Chendo to ask him what was happening to Uicho. Chendo told him that Uicho had all the dinner time standing there without moving and that he better help him with the mortar to finish placing the stones on the facade.

Philip could not stand the desire to know what was going through Uicho's mind and walked towards Uicho without hesitating a moment of his own ability to create anything like any man.

Philip stood on Uicho's right side, who immediately noticed Philip's presence, but said nothing, only followed him with his gaze, as Philip walked down the slope, who unmistakably said:

"It is going to fall." Uicho nodded his head in sign of approval.

"We will do what the engineer said, let us do our part and see what the hell happens," Uicho said.

Philip had no choice but to accept what the foreman said because he was right that the engineer was the head of the work.

And that they, having to comply with their obligations, should abide by his orders. For that, Philip kept his idea of intervening, submitting to his rightful place as the mason's assistant. He did not mention a word all afternoon, and he did not even say a single word on the way back to the dump.

He returned to his hut very seriously without even saying good-bye to others. Elida received him with some serenity because she sensed what had happened, that she embraced him by kissing him very passionately, as usual, taking him to the bed to be with him. Philip let himself be carried away by his detachment from the circumstances, and the intention was reciprocated.

"What you need is love," Elida told him.

In the following days, they took care of founding the entrance so that in a few weeks they could finish all that part of the construction. Meanwhile, Philip visited The Old Lady with the White Hair in search of more answers, whenever he had a chance.

On Saturdays, they worked no more until noon, but with the workload they left not before six o'clock in the afternoon, trying to finish as soon as possible. On Sundays, he just wanted to be with his beloved, and help her with those things that women cannot do, according to him. She liked to be very independent, she always had a good time fixing and moving things in the hut to make it more comfortable for them.

Elida took the time to improve all possible aspects of the hut without falling into ostentatious aspects. Rather, her idea was very practical and simple, which was reflected in her person transforming everything she touched into something alive, useful, and practical. The idea of water harvesting by passing it through carbon filters was somewhat innovative for that time, among other things she did for her pimps. In general, she always did it to whoever asked, she was always fixing things in other huts along with her soul friends. Philip was surprised to see how the view of the place changed in a way that everything was filled with light, with vents everywhere, which she controlled with some ropes, along with some cans of beans she used as pulleys, to open and close the holes with small doors that she had invented with garbage remains.

There were things that Philip still ignored from her, but with time he was discovering everything for which he always loved her, the best she could be herself. That was the reason why he loved her, for being herself. Faithful to her being, without hesitation in the love of her heart, despite the many trials that she had to live. Philip loved her and was willing to give his life for them, for her, and for the new being who had gestated with their naked love, without prejudices or conditions, openly in mutual agreement.

At times he was distressed by the idea of inheriting the world he had from that innocent being. He did not refer to the world of misery. Well, that is where simplicity makes sense. He was referring to social injustice, gender inequality, to machismo, as much as feminism and all the misunderstandings that lead everyone to fall into conflict with others.

Philip knew that he could not change the whole world to leave a better one for his offspring. He could never with the powerful and their means of dragging, that we all accept comfortably and without hesitation. What could a poor beggar do against world power and its entertainment system, how could he draw everyone's attention to convince them of something they do wrong? If everyone has already fallen into the belief of the lie. No one would listen to a poor beggar pointing out the faults that are committed in society because there would be prejudices that would prevent individuals from becoming aware of their own faults; and in that way, they would condemn Philip's idea to one more label. Just like society uses its stereotypes to refer to ideas that do not fit in the conventional, to the condemnation of the idealistic dreamer.

All these waves of the sea of thought tired Philip's consciousness, giving him an attack of anxiety whenever he thought about it. He knew well how to clear up the confusion, no matter where, he got away a moment from everyone so that he could meditate a little on the torture that the mind creates by fear.

It is almost impossible for a man to save the world because greed and indifference blind men from the truth about humility, set them apart from compassion that is transformed by the service to others, along with many other things that prevent the inner awakening of consciousness. We already had examples of teachers who tried to teach us the tools to discover ourselves internally, then return as a different being to the outside. Being so, it is a reliable way for the misunderstandings that generate conflict between individuals, but most people only take the ideas that suit their interests.

There are many reasons why men, are not interested in clarifying our misunderstandings, not just with others but with ourselves.

Philip recalled the words of The Old Lady with the White Hair about social justice, mutual respect, and self-respect.

Philip believed that with love everything would be solved in the world because in true love there is no envy, nor doubts, much less greed; for, in love we live for others, to serve in the way that we would like to be served, with the same respect and compassion without expecting anything in return because if that, would be vanity too.

All this philosophy of love and freedom that the Old Lady tried to convey to him in every session that Philip could attend, coincided with his convictions about life in general, both earthly and spiritual. Perhaps, he was not yet ready to understand the condition he inherited from his father, which made him noble in a way and deserving of the award of truth, which every man eager to power would like to be to profit from it. Such as it happens in this age.

In the rush to finish the work as soon as possible, the foreman did not allow them to take rest for more than an hour. They were supposed to take only half an hour and stay close to the construction so they could get back to work as soon as possible. But, already tired of the frustrating situation that caused him to think that they built foolishness that would collapse; perhaps, on top of themselves, he let them go at noon.

"Enough!" Uicho screamed, throwing the tools in his hand on the ground, and, turning to see Chendo, asked him to leave, just like everyone else. "Get it, my Chendo. Go away boys, take an hour, you deserve it." They all went very happily to the places they had already conditioned to share their food among them. There were some days they had left food for later. Well, sharing multiplies everything the heart wants to give. Give and it will multiply, serve and you will be served with the same respect; love, but do not expect anything in return.

Philip did not want to miss the moment to visit the Old Lady and find out more about that place that he found fascinating. He wanted to know about the mystery of the blue stone, which emitted that subliminal light that made him feel attracted to it. He wanted to know the mystery of the spear and the medallion, and what was represented for the civilization that was annihilated by their own creator; but above all, he wanted to know what role they could play today.

Philip thought something that made him feel uncomfortable, a little arrogant and vicious, thinking that perhaps they would serve to subdue the foolish wicked to realize their ingratitude with all the good and sacredness of the planet. For, all souls are sacred, ignorance is what blinds them.

He wanted to free himself from the torment that his own mind was causing him, by clinging to an idea that perhaps he did not understand, so he rushed to arrive as soon as possible to try to get some information out of The Old Lady with the White Hair.

It was clear that he did not know how to handle his impetus of courage in the best way so that his mind would not be filled with the suggestive hell that formed his fears, his helplessness for leaving a better world for his offspring. For so, he thought that those mysterious objects would help him with the purpose that had been born in his heart when he found out that he would be a father.

Philip got a little agitated by how fast he was going and stood at the entrance to get some air. She waited for him sitting on the stone as she always did, but this time the stone did not radiate any light, which was strange to Philip. He did not ask a word and he immediately sat in front of her, while the Old Lady pointed the spear at him right in his chest.

"Why do you want to change the world?" The Old Lady asked him.

"If you all tried to change some things," Philip answered.

In that, the Old Lady interrupted him by saying:

"To be like you?"

He was silent not knowing how to explain to the Old Lady what he really wanted, but she knew what his heart suffered by not receiving recognition for his work, the prestige that any nobleman receives for his education or performance in service, that Philip imagined at times for himself. The Old Lady calmed his anxiety a bit by touching his forehead with her left hand.

Philip felt confident to ask the Old Lady about the spear, but the Old Lady interrupted him with a story about a door unknown by ignorance, which is closer than you think. To open it, it would need a key that only the chosen one owns, to intervene at the precise time.

"When you enter you will understand who to intervene in," the Old Lady told him, after telling him the story about the door.

Philip wanted to know what those mysterious artifacts were for and now the Old Lady gave him another one of her labyrinths to think about. Or is it that, she put him on alert about something that he should contemplate among his concerns for wanting to know more about things that Philip was not prepared yet, as to manage the power generated by the understanding of the door and *The Tools of Order*?

"You must overcome greed before moving forward in your next step," the Old Lady told him.

"Nothing I have. I am not interested in riches. I believe that capitalism is the one that marginalizes and deprives," Philip replied. In that, the Old Lady approached him with a bowl in her hand containing a yellow powder, which she blew on Philip's face. Philip began to cough by drowning himself unable to breathe. Believing that he would die, kneels in front of the Old Lady seeing her in the eyes, while images of certain situations that could happen in his life were coming to mind. He could not tell the details because the flashes passed very quickly, and he had to deal with trying to breathe to save his life.

In that, The Old Lady with the White Hair put the spear on his chest, and he stopped coughing, being able to breathe normally. He stood up at once feeling very calm, understanding within himself some things, but still intended to want to know more.

When Philip walked to leave back to work, the Old Lady told him:

"Greed is a poison that pollutes the souls of men. Don't forget."Philip did not understand what role the words of the Old Lady played in his life. He just turned around and went back to work.

Back at the construction site, Philip immediately searched the Saint to find out if he could help him with some of his concerns, but he could not find him anywhere. He realized that Raziel, the other beggar who lived in the dumpster, was not around either. He went to ask Chendo if he had seen him, so Chendo told him that they had gone to their private session. Philip found the tone in which Chendo had referred regarding the private session somewhat funny, for as he was always very joking, he had said it in a very candid way.

"What is that?"

Chendo told him that they went every month on that date to the chapel of the neighboring village where the foreman lived, for a reading of a book. He told him that Uicho had taken them, that he would return later, and that he had already left instructions to finish with the facade.

Philip was still somewhat confused by the effect of the mysterious dust, hence did not know what to do. He stood thinking of the words the Old Lady had told him; besides, the mystery of the door and its mysterious key. "Go on, fool. He said he will come back in two hours and then we'll go home," Chendo told him.

Philip had no choice but to deal with what was his due, going to help him with the facade to advance on as much as they could before the foreman returned. Even so, there were things that troubled him and debated in thought as he worked, trying to understand things with what he already knew.

He had read about the Philosopher's Stone and other objects that men coveted to take the power they wielded, and he refused to believe, despite what he had already experienced in the supernatural. It seemed absurd to him that such objects with powers over men existed.

Although the idea seemed somewhat tempting, that of possessing such objects to suppress the injustice of fools and greedy, and then give a better world to his loved ones.

Philip had long since lost faith in religion and doubted the God who had exterminated his own creation. That made him feel resentment thinking of the lost dreams of those souls, in the agony of their lives by not finding an answer to the call of mercy.

Philip thought that, perhaps, the lesson the teacher was trying to give to his creation was not entirely successful, due to the lack of approximation from the teacher to teach the truth to the ignorant. That, for so the student was not guilty, the teacher had failed in the way to approach the student, leaving him adrift in the delights of the flesh. And that The Creator, in an attack of anger for not paying attention to them, decided to annihilate them. Philip took pains to learn as much as he could in every matter possible, to seek to fill the gap left by the divine at the time they decide that we should live, which in a way, is the silence they agreed with each other about our destiny.

The God that man tries to make for himself demands submission, is jealous, and threatens not only carnal death, spiritual death too. Condemning the bad students to the perpetual punishment according to their lack, as a petty vice that punishes and awards others at once without any remorse.

The foreman had returned sooner than they had anticipated. Philip was thinking all that was neglected by forgetting some stones that Chendo had told him he had to bring to put them on the facade, but by not doing so they could not finish in time. Uicho realized that, but without the intention of claiming something he called them to go home with a cry; so, everyone was surprised to hear it, they just stared at him and did nothing for a moment. He had to yell at them again so everyone could hurry to store the tools in the room Uicho used as an office to keep the blueprint.

The village was lost from sight on the horizon at the time Philip was trying to leave behind the thoughts of his mystery, to welcome the desire to see his beloved. Thinking about how to do so that she had the easiest things while he went to work.

"The key," said the other young mysterious man in a low voice, but enough for Philip to hear it, who immediately turned to see him in the eye.

"Man, you too? My dear," Chendo said, moving his head back and forth.

Raziel's other young companion looked at him with a smile that almost came out of his face. Same Chendo, and at the same time they let out a laugh. Philip only winced a little with his face, like a feigned smile; for, what that young man had said seemed strange to him, for he stared at the young man as he was talking with Chendo. Thinking of how likely it would be for this young man to know about the key, or that he mentioned it at that very moment. What a cheeky coincidence that he played with his mind, that he made him investigate the possible answers for what that young man had mentioned as the key.

In one of his many insistences on accommodating such a mention, Philip remembered Elida and her passionate kisses, which suddenly forgot everything else. At that moment, the young man looked him in the eye. Chendo continued as if he were talking to him, but the young man looked at Philip the moment he sighed for Elida.

"Love," Philip thought.

He could not bear the urge to tell Elida about The Old Lady with the White Hair and her magical powders that almost killed him, of what had happened to the foreman, the mystery of Raziel and the Saint. In addition, many other things had been abundantly surpassed in his thought, in a way that he kept talking.

Elida was preparing a hen along with her pimps, but these left immediately when they saw Philip enter. Well, Carmela when she saw him, thought her husband had come back too. Inés was melting down when she see them together, maybe because she envied in a good way the love they radiated, that she stayed stoned as bewitched. Carmela had to pull her by the hand, as usual.

Elida looked at him very attentively as she plucked the hen, and she just stopped seeing him for a moment to make sure she did not burn with the hot water when pulling the feathers. There are times when we need to let go of some things that happen to us, to release any doubts about the experience; for that, Philip was trying to get out a little of what his mind constantly overstepped. Elida left the hen for a moment inside the vase to go give him a kiss, being the only way for him to stop talking. Philip just stared at her without saying anything. Then, she came back to pull the last feathers of the hen before the water cooled down and it was harder to pull them.

"Maybe I thought I made paella for my walking Quixote and this one came something earlier than usual. Why do not you go do something out there? Tell Inés and Mama Chayo to come, that there are still things to do, that they better stop being pimped that this does not prepare itself. Come on, and do not be late," Elida told him, while Philip was just looking at her with a big smile that came upon his face.

Understanding the situation and taking his share, he went looking for Chendo to see if they went hunting with the children.

As he left the hut, he saw Inés and Carmela, who they called Mama Chayo, returning to the hut to continue helping Elida. Philip only greeted them as he passed. The lady had to pull Inés to get into the hut.

Chendo and the children were already almost departing to go hunting, along with the other young man who worked with them on the construction site. The moment Philip approached they filled their water bottles, they kept in their backpacks a little pepper and salt in case they were lucky in the hunt, which was almost always some country rats or prairie rabbits.

"Let's go, fool," Chendo told him when he saw him. Philip returned to take a bow of arrows that his father had left him, which was kept in one of his secret trunks, along with some arrows with black tips, with the feathers used to give it aerodynamic stability in purple.

A leather satchel along with his water bottle was loaded, and the six went to form memories in the children, lessons for adults, and life for all.

They had to walk for more than half an hour to get to the place where Chendo was taking them hunting because he said that in that place there was not yet the voracity of some people who have consistently fed the inconsiderate destruction of forests, the sea, and the fertile land. Chendo, in a different way, made his children understand, as they walked along a sidewalk towards a few small hills.

Philip and the other young man delayed a little walking behind them, while the oldest of the three children asked their father about things he had done before the other two were born.

"Is it true, dad, that you killed a deer one time?"

"Yeah, it was big," Chendo answered.

"I told you all," told the boy to his two brothers.

They were very astonished to hear it, and they were very proud of their father, that they begged him immediately to tell them how it had happened.

Philip tried to find the reason why his destiny showed him that example of an ordinary man with his children, teaching them how good can be obtained without harming any ecosystem. At least that is how he understood it.

While Chendo recounted that great feat, Philip asked the other young man who walked with him for his name:

"What is your name?" Philip asked him a little sorry

"In the morning when the sun rises, what is the first thing you do Philip?" the young man said before answering his name.

Philip stared into his eyes and could see a strange light in them that was illuminated when he asked that. And the other young man stared at him too.

"Gabriel," said the young man.

"Nice to meet you," said Philip.

They chatted for a good time on the way until they passed the little hills, and they came to a valley where there was a lot of vegetation with all kinds of fruits, and animals that Philip nor the children had seen before. There were birds of all kinds flying over their heads.

Chendo suddenly stopped somewhat astonished, for it was not the place he had visited before, that immediately turned to see Gabriel. Well, they had gone hunting together with the children down that course a few days ago. But then he thought that maybe they had strayed down another sidewalk before passing the hills because it was not explained how he had not realized that place after so many times going down that course.

That is the same place, where Philip knew a cave where his dad took him when he was a kid to tell him stories his grandfather had told him. For so Philip was not surprised to have reached that mystical place.

Chendo could not see the horizon due to so much vegetation, that he had to climb a stone to see how big the place was. To his surprise, was bigger than he imagined, and that surprised him more because it was not possible that this place was on the other side of the hills because you could see it from anywhere without having to pass the hills according to the dimension that place had. But it was not so because, before passing the hills, you could not see anything, it was just as you pass the hills that you could enter that little paramo of paradise.

As they entered a little, they reached where a small stream of crystal-clear water was, where you could see the fish swim quietly. When they saw that stream, they all ran to get into it. When they realized that the fish did not run away from them, they were a little scared, but immediately felt very confident and cheerful, so they began to play among themselves as if time did not pass.

Gabriel slowly entered the stream with his hands outstretched to be able to touch the water with the tip of his fingers. Then the fish began to circulate around him, and the children kept saying that they wanted to do so too. So Gabriel nodded that they could try. As the children put their hands in the water, the fish began to circulate around them as well.

Philip and Chendo, when they saw what happened, soon tried to, but the fish did not circulate around them. Instead, three fish suddenly appeared in front of each of them as an offering in sacrifice, which they took out of the water to take them away.

As they prepared to return after the children managed to get out of the water because it was a difficult thing to convince them to leave that joy, they felt while playing with Gabriel and the fish in the stream; Gabriel asked them to stay a little longer so they could cook three of the six fish they had offered themselves to slaughter. Then, Philip remembered that Elida was preparing the hen for dinner; so, he suggested that they should be taken back. Gabriel insisted once more, this time touching Philip's shoulder with his hand, who immediately felt a great peace within him, which made him forget all concern about what was happening on the other side of the hills.

Philip helped Gabriel to light the fire by rubbing one stick with another until they formed a small ember to throw in the candela they had already prepared, while the children were looking for some branches to contribute. Chendo prepared the fish by removing its guts and scales and strung them on a stick so he could easily turn them over.

They all gathered around the fire pit telling stories as the fish cooked slowly in the fire. It seemed that time did not pass, having a feeling of not wanting to go anywhere, just being there in that beautiful paradise that gave them eating without resistance.

After a good time of lunch and children playing around, Philip was left thinking with a lost gaze as if trying to remember something he had to do. Looking at the embers that had remained, he remembered that Elida had told him not to be long for dinner, so he called everyone to go back, and they immediately gathered around Gabriel, intuiting that he knew the way back to guide them.

By the time Gabriel began walking, he asked them to pick up some legumes to take home, which they all did by casting only what fit them in their backpacks. Lettuce and carrots grew by the side of the road, plus many more legumes that they did not recognize. In an orderly and respectful manner, they took each one's own thing without damaging the plants that were next to them. Although it appeared to be a garden and had no linear or specific order indicating any groove made by someone, all legumes were scrambled between them, but with a rational position that divided them by species.

Those that required more moisture grew next to the stream, and those that required a certain level of moisture or drainage were accommodated in ideal positions where the earth was accommodated for rooting; and so, each plant settled in the exact place to grow in a harmonious way, in a self-sustaining ecosystem. At least that seemed to Philip by observing so much order where anyone would think it is chaos. Such as in the woods, so neat was that place but in a higher way, with more beauty and purpose. He could also see a few small mounds that stood out everywhere with watermelon plants in each of them, which could be seen from two or three watermelons per plant.

Philip realized that there were insects that only ate specific plants separated between the legumes without damaging any tuber or leaf of any of the edible legumes for men. He thought it was a dream come true, those that he had always idealized, but that reality prevented him for many reasons that he could not overcome.

From how excited he was, as he went on to the entrance of the place, he forgot to pay attention to the road, letting pass some details that could serve him later, if he intended to return another time with

Elida and to be able to show her that beautiful dream place, which was very close to the dump where they came. Almost is another irony that we do not fully understand in its essence, nor in the purpose of why we live so close to paradise without realizing it. Because we prefer to fight for a purpose that has been instilled in us, a dream that has been suggested according to the model that has been imposed on each age. Some technological development, in a way, makes us forget about who we really are, keeping us engaged in a distraction specifically machined, according to the susceptibility of each of us who live in this reality.

Philip did not realize that they had left the hills due to certain plants that blocked his view next to the road, but that they were gradually yielding. When they were far enough, only some small shrubs remained in that desolate paramo, which after a few minutes he was recognized. He was able to see in the distance the hole where the dump was.

In front of Philip was Chendo hugging his children, singing and laughing very cheerfully, not being worried about anything.

For this, Gabriel walked behind them. Philip could not stand the urge to turn back to see, so he could remember the way back to paradise. Trying to locate the entrance between the hills, he could not recognize any detail, which he found strange because they seemed as if they were not the same hills. Nor could he ensure with certainty where the entrance was. Well, no vestige of the vegetation could see anywhere. Not being even so far away that they left that area. It was supposed that it was possible to see such a splendid place at that distance, due to the magnitude that was appreciated from within.

Although Philip knew that he had never seen it before, for he visited the cave on that course, but never got to that place hidden before everyone's eyes. He did not quite understand how he could not see it before. Also, his father had never mentioned among his stories that the place was so splendid as to go unnoticed and being so close to the dump.

"Look in your heart," said Gabriel while Philip was trying to see where the entrance had possibly been.

He immediately turned all his attention to Gabriel when he heard him say that, and he stopped, feeling a tremendous desire to cry when he saw him in the eye, feeling the depths of his message. Now he touched his chest with his right hand. Gabriel caught up with him and hugged him, for which Philip felt much better, somewhat contented, carefree of what had happened. Then, the two walked together behind Chendo and the children, who were making songs of praise to the all-powerful high in the sky with uncontrollable ecstasy.

All those things that he talked to Gabriel as they walked the sidewalk back to the dump, Philip said were things that everyone must live to know. Well, no one could teach you better than you what you need, what you feel or dream of, no one knows how your mind is lost in the deep sea of thought, nor how your dreams are drowned in hopelessness, or how much the wound hurts. That, the details corresponded to each one, in the time that they had to live in this reality. Being essential to take advantage of the lesson that these details teach us in life so that we can find the reasons for many of our doubts, as the key to overcoming fear that prevents spiritual growth in each of us so that we can advance in the reunion with the truth that lies within each one.

As they approached the dump, the sidewalk was enlarged to form a dirt road with some stones sticking out everywhere, making Philip feel more familiar with the place when he recognized the terrain. Then the fears went out of his mind, feeling a little carefree about wanting to return to that place, for his thoughts were immediately dealt with by his reality in recognizing the return to the dump.

Somehow, he was returning to his mental reality, so that the sea of thought began to work on the paella that Elida was preparing, besides that he was more eager to see her. Although his emotion faded, he still tried to rescue what he could by seeing the joy of the children playing and singing praises to their father, without looking like they would stop the ecstasy they had discovered in them at some point. Philip watched them behind them, walking with Gabriel with the amber of the sunset on their backs. That way, they returned to the dump chasing their shadows when they ended their hunting adventure.

Chapter 6
The Black Bird

Upon arriving at the dump, each one said goodbye to their own way when they reached where their respective huts were. Philip was the last to reach his hut after having taken a moment thinking some things. Well, a few steps before he reaches the hut, Philip managed to see Chendo and the children, enter their hut with the same enthusiasm they had along the way. He heard Mama Chayo yelling at them to leave so much fuss and go handwash because dinner was ready. He wondered what was special about that scene in his life, and if it would be useful in his personal path. Without finding the reason for what he was a witness, he turned around and went to his hut.

Philip arrived with the enthusiasm to tell Elida about some things that had happened, but she interrupted him by telling him to go wash his hands because dinner was ready. Philip upon hearing her had no objection, doing as she had indicated to him. He was trying to tell her something before he forgot, but she insisted on him in such a way that he could not refuse her, he was following everything she asked of him, completely forgetting everything he had been through; besides how glad he was to see her, that he lost now all vestige in his mind of that paradise.

He kept seeing the tasty paella that was served on the table while washing his hands, that when he finished immediately ran to sit as if he were very hungry. Congratulating Elida for all that she had done and admiring how all the food looked. Philip had never eaten so much in his life, that he was pleased more than anything else.

Elida stared at him while she was standing on the other side of the table, very serious. Philip quickly reacted by getting up to give her a kiss, and he carried her by giving her a spin in the air.

Philip asked her where she had got so many things if she had done all that alone and if she had already rested enough in the day because of her pregnancy, among other things. Elida had to interrupt him by telling him that it was time to share the moment together without any doubt that could ruin the occasion. Well, she had decided to tell him about her past after dinner.

"What is it? what is the matter with you skinny?"

"I'll tell you something I've remembered," Elida replied.

She insisted that they enjoy the food and the moment, that everything comes in its time without delay, without forcing events. Philip perfectly understood the reason for her insistence and respected her decision he got carried away taking advantage of the moment to enjoy with her the occasion.

She asked him about how he had done at work, while they ate the paella delicacy she had prepared in detail and care throughout the afternoon. Philip began to tell her what had happened at work, of why they had left early that day.

At that moment, he remembered the fish he brought in the backpack, immediately going to put them in a bucket of water. They were surprised to see that the fish swam into the bucket as soon as he had thrown them out, without explaining to himself how possible was for them to remain alive. Philip was unaware of any doubt knowing that everything was possible at that point in his life and set out to make a small well to throw the fish to be reproduced, for which Elida hugged him and kissed him all over the face very glad that they would have a self-sustaining resource, for that she agreed to contribute to the project that Philip had thought of. Philip told her that she could not make efforts because of her pregnancy, that she would better worry about feeding them to grow up, and that he would take care of the heaviest.

Elida was a very independent woman who never expected others to do things for her, or that others said she cannot do something on her own, she did not feel worthy of consideration. She said that it was disrespectful to people, and that is why she was always trying to help others without caring that she was pregnant. Elida was well cared for by her pimps, whom she loved as if they were from her own family.

Well, somehow, it was the only thing closest that she had resembling the affection that is felt in the home. They always took care of her, although she insisted that she could do it alone while pregnant, that this was not a pretext to work on what she could; also, it would be an example for babies if the mother was proactive and productive.

Elida told Philip that between the three they had helped each other prepare dinner in each of the three huts, that always supported each other when they needed something, and that he should not worry as much about how she could manage on her own with the pregnancy, that she was female enough to know how to manage the situation.

She asked him to trust her and told him that she would never leave him under any circumstances for which Philip was very serious thinking about the reasons she might have to say such a thing, that he just stared at her a little worried.

He stood in front of the wood that covered the entrance, staring towards the hole where the winter equinox light entered, recalling the night she came into his life, with a melancholy tone on his face for the fear of losing them, for some reason that the divine might have for the spirits of each. Without knowing what to do against such a decision, his heart was broken imagining the loss of those he loved. He did not understand the reason for having them and then losing them for a reason that was not involved in the plans of the living.

Elida, seeing the tone of anguish on his face, holds him by his hands and took him to sit with her on the bed, staring into his eyes. Philip, recognizing the look of sincerity that he loved in her, let himself be carried away by a feeling of trust that he felt when he looked at her, forgetting the fears for an instant.

Elida told him that her mother was born on a farm near Pueblito Blanco, in Andalusia, Spain. That her grandpa had brought them to the Americas because of political problems. By the boldness of an individual who proclaimed himself 'Leader of Spain by the hand of God. She told him that Grandpa differed from his ideals and that is why they had to flee their home, like many more at that time but they had to shut up for fear.

The grandfather, in addition to being a civil engineer, was one of the most recognized architects around the world. That is why in America, they received him with great enthusiasm. Well, the style of his work stood out by how he mixed the design with the natural environment of the place, taking advantage of the natural resources for the construction. Giving it a very local sense, that People identified with those places where nature could grow in a harmonious sense with society.

Grandpa had contributed to the design of many of the most beautiful buildings in some cities in Europe. It had been because of oppression so he left his house and friends, having to run away with only what they were wearing that day. The grandmother followed him along with her three children, Elida's mother and two young children who grew up in an atmosphere of honesty and great opulence, due to the success of grandpa because they never lacked anything; also, Grandma was a great woman and painter well-known, with enough resources to not depend on anyone.

Although on this new continent they had been equal to or more successful than in the old, they always sought to teach their children the humility of service to others, as well as respect for nature, honesty, and sincerity of word.

Philip listened very surprisedly to all that Elida told him about her family, and how grandparents had taught their children the ideals he felt his own in his heart, that tears almost came to him knowing that such a thing was possible.

Elida told him that her grandparents served the community in the villages near the city where they lived, helping the parishes of the villages with food and things for those in need. Themselves served without people knowing that it was them who provided things. They mixed as volunteers to serve to eat and distribute clothes to the people. Grandma oversaw handing out to women and children.

Grandma was a very quaint and carefree woman of what people might think or say of her. When she spoke, she did it in a very cheerful way, with great enthusiasm, almost to the point of shouting as she spoke. She tried the clothes along with the ladies and girls of the villages they visited and gave them health and personal hygiene advice. She wore somewhat tousled short hair, with a purple head-band, a flowered dress of many colors every time they were going to serve the community.

Same the children, they dressed as simple that made them feel comfortable with what they did, so as not to make others feel bad in fancy clothes or things like that. They handed things out to the children, to whom they came to take a great affection for many of them, and of whom they became very good friends.

As children were very young when they arrived from Spain, all these great examples became their favorite custom, helping with joy and joy of the heart. To the extent of waiting for the weekend to go out to the villages to help others and be able to visit their friends, they loved so much, without any prejudice, without any ambition.

Seeing their parents' passionate dedication to helping others, along with the great joy they discovered in doing it themselves, they understood that service to others was something that filled them with great satisfaction in their hearts; for neither money nor opulence attracted them more like service and giving to those in need, as well as the friendship and appreciation of the people.

Elida told him that her grandpa had given a wagon with a mule to a gentleman who greatly appreciated and with whom he made a great friendship, and always procured him in as much time as possible in his life, whom he came to love as a brother.

They were never treated with suspicion or discrimination, nor did anyone ever feel less than any of them. On the contrary, all people loved them as if they were part of their community, and they always emphasized that they were part of the same community as them, the human community.

The great joy of living with them made them forget the occasion that they were rich, almost wanting to stay with them forever. But they belonged to a level that society delimits, and in which they had their home. Of course, they would stay, if possible as Grandma once said, but it was true that she would not leave her family for anything because she would follow her husband forever wherever he goes without hesitation.

Elida was thinking about the last words she had mentioned, with her gaze lost at some point in the past she had remembered. Philip realized her melancholy that almost turned her into tears, he hugged her next to his chest telling her he would always be with them no matter what might happen. Looking her in the eye, he took her face with his hands and told her that he loved her, that she was her moon and his star, and the sprinkle of dawn.

Both touched Elida's belly with great tenderness and love, that the product of their love jumped suddenly, stretching as far as it could, being able to clearly see one of the baby's feet pushing Elida's belly almost at the height of the heart.

"I love you," they both said at the same time; then they kissed as they laughed for having agreed on what their hearts had felt. By the way, the senses and emotions are synchronized, by living the same intention in the awakening of the inner being, coinciding with love.

The next day, Philip got up very early picking things up around the hut, trying to leave as little as possible on his rightful part according to his habits in the chore of his home, so she would not try too hard during the workday, which kept him busy away from her and their baby who was on the way.

On Sunday morning, Elida got up very early preparing some bags with some food and filling two bottles with water. Philip awoke by the noise she made in the kitchen, which seemed a bit strange to him because on Sundays they would wake up a little late, that is why he got up somewhat puzzled.

As soon as she saw him, Elida asked him to take her to the chapel in the nearest village, which was the same village where Uicho lived, the foreman of the construction site.

"For what, or what?"

"I want to visit a friend," Elida told him.

Philip was staring at her from head to toe, looking for an instant on Elida's belly, then he looked her in the eye. Not finding any malice in her eyes, he recognized the emotion of sincerity in her, that he could only say:

"Yes skinny, let me see what I can do." He put on the most decent thing he found among his rags to go out and get Chendo because he was the only one who had a mule cart at the dump, he wanted to ask him if he could take them as a favor.

"Maybe," Chendo told him. "Well, it is more than two hours." Mama Chayo had listened as they chatted, and came out immediately telling Chendo to take them because Elida had a diligence to do very important to her life in that village.

He did not have to beg much because Chendo appreciated Philip in a very good way, who have not hesitated to offer to take them.

On Sundays, when they were not helping their women, or since they were children and they would not collect among the piles of garbage, they always spent it together wherever they went. Except when Chendo started working and Philip still did not know whether to venture out of his security zone; or perhaps, he dared not go out because of the insecurity that the fears had caused in him, after losing a piece of his soul whit the death of his parents.

Chendo took the reins of the mule, and Philip accompanied him in front along with Chendo's eldest son, who sat in the middle of the two, just as was his custom when riding in the wagon with his father. Elida and Mama Chayo carried the other two little ones with them in the back along with the bags that each had prepared beforehand, as among them they had already agreed, having everything ready for the journey. In this way, they gathered their destinies in a single journey, for reasons no mortal man could suspect, as some still cannot understand the meaning of the union.

"Sustained in your arms, we travel together in the infinity, in this astral instant," Philip said quietly, as the stars began to fade out of view due to the sunrise that overshadowed its farthest sisters with its light.

"That was good, fool," Chendo told him in a very candid manner.

The boy started at him with a big smile and nodded as a sign of approval of what Philip had said.

The transition of the early morning lasted enough for them to enjoy the sunrise, loaded with rays of light on the clouds that were in the distance, giving them shape and color as the rain of energy expanded, which clarified every face of creation.

Already entered the road, the two little ones had fallen asleep because Mama Chayo had woken them up very early to get ready.

The oldest of the kids had to help them get dressed, so half asleep they were. That is why they did not have their normal sleep hours and the sunrise lulled them even more, that they huddled with Elida on each side of her belly.

Counting endless stories, all three of them were leading the wagon, and in one of those stories that Chendo told, the little one pulled his arm with which he was in charge, insinuating him to ask Philip about what he had told him one day about him.

"Dad, dad, tell him," said the boy quietly, pointing his head towards Philip who turned to see Chendo asking him what the little one meant.

Chendo, without letting go of the rein at any time, looked in his memory to which part of Philip's story his son referred, and he did not take long to sense the part he always insisted on telling him repeatedly.

"About the black bird," Chendo said, turning to see Philip.

Philip was a little surprised that the little one was struck by the tale of the black bird so much that he had no choice but to tell him what had happened to him that autumn afternoon.

Having Philip three years or so, a strange bird had stood outside the hut's window where he slept, while his parents were on the other side of the hut looking for some things to fill the gaps as much as possible with materials they had found among the rubbish since in the winter it got a little cold in that part of the country.

It was his mother who, by female intuition, felt a pressure on her chest that alerted her in a sign that something bad was going on with her son, for she rushed out immediately around the hut to find out what it was. A black bird of unknown appearance, perched on the eucalyptus outside the window where Philip slept. It scared her in such a way that she cried terrified of the impression of the look that the creature had. Reacting immediately, she crawled out the window to take her son in her arms so that he would not be hurt by that strange creature.

His father arrived immediately with a piece of wood in his hand that he had picked up in the race when he heard the cries of Philip's mother, just as that strange bird pounced upon Philip, the same moment her mom jumped over the window to stop it.

With a certain hit on one of its wings, Philip's father stopped it before it came to touch either of them, which made the creature complain in a very strange way. Scaring Philip's mother even more, who screamed with great terror. His mother awoke him by taking him quickly in her arms, and Philip could see the eyes of that creature staring at him. Just before it left the place, flapping its wings with great force, which even toss Philip's father to the ground, also having torn the curtains with the force of its flutter. Fallen on the ground, Philip's dad could hear how that creature complained, as it got lost in the clouds. It was like a person who screamed in a strange language, that gave him goosebumps and ran out, rushing into the hut to see if that strange creature had done anything to them.

The mother was still in a fit of hysteria from the impression, looking everywhere screaming to leave them alone, unable to control herself. The father came in as scared as the mom, but he felt a great relief to see that nothing had happened to them and ran to hug them right away, kissing them both on the forehead.

That had certainly left sequels difficult to forget in all of them, but more in Philip because he had to live many years before he ceased to have nightmares about the eyes of that creature.

The boy was so scared that his eyes were coming out, and he clung to his dad's arm while watching Philip say that story, which somehow, served to distract him along the way, for they were about to reach the village at the time when he finished saying, "I think I never stopped remembering, even on some nights I dream about it."

The barking of dogs woke the children, and they began to ask what was going on, so the mom gladly them a little bit telling them they had already arrived. Being the children very happy to remember that they were on that adventure of visiting another village for the first time.

Three blocks from the chapel where they were going, Philip reached The Zorro parked as three houses on the corner. Upon Chendo noticing, he told him that that was the foreman's house. As he had already gone many times to that village since his grandfather had inherited the wagon from him, he already knew where Uicho lived.

The dogs followed the wagon until they reached the chapel, along with some curious children who joined, greeting the little ones. They asked each other their names, and where they came from, among other things. The little ones were very happy to be able to meet other children. When the children of the village asked them where they were going, the oldest of the three responded that they were going to the chapel. There were people peeking out the window when they heard the barking of the dogs and the screams of the children. Also, two old men who were on either side of the street were prostrate on the ground as they passed through the place. They were even surprised to see them prostrate ignoring the reason why they were bowing.

"Sure, everyone has his madness in this life," Elida said as Philip turned to see her.

She looked at him too smiling at him with great charisma, and she tossed him a kiss with her hand, which he caught with his hand and put it in his heart now they stopped, to then finally disembark in front of the chapel.

Felipe helped get down Mama Chayo along with the children, and Mama Chayo with Philip, they lowered Elida carefully from the wagon, while Chendo held the reins so that the mule would not walk. The oldest of the three children, as always, was next to his father learning the maneuver. So Chendo taught him how to pull the rein so that the mule would not walk while the others were getting off. Elida, now stepped on the ground rushed into the chapel, which was immediately followed by Felipe, Mama Chayo, and the two young children.

Elida entered and walked towards the altar slowly, being able to see the priest who was in front of that man nailed to the cross. "Only man and his God," the priest whispered, while Elida was getting close enough to hear him.

"Father Joaquin," Elida told him.

The priest turned around immediately upon recognizing that voice and was watching her for a moment very surprised.

"My child!" the father said.

"Uncle Joaquin," Elida told him, crying disconsolately.

He immediately hugged her tightly, asking her a lot of things about what had happened to her, where she had been all that time that she had disappeared.

Father Joaquin told her that everyone had thought that she had died after searching for her for more than a year and a half by the authorities, thanks to Grandma's insistence because at one point the authorities did not want to look any further. Her Grandma had to hire a private investigator to continue her search.

Father Joaquin never imagined finding her so far from where she had disappeared. He was very excited that he let go of the cry when he realized she was pregnant, filling her with kisses and praise as if she were a girl.

He immediately insisted that they should notify the family, arguing that Grandma was very concerned that she had not found any trace of her all that time, then he told them that she would be very happy to know that she was okay. Also, they should notify the competent authorities of her whereabouts. Elida interrupted him at the time asking him to go to a more private place to tell him what had happened to her, and the reasons she had to not say anything about where she was.

Father Joaquin asked them to accompany him to the sacristy so that they would rest a little from the journey. Calling the sacristan with his hand, told them, "Come, come, I imagine you want something to eat."

He requested the sacristan and a lady who cooked him every day in the chapel that they bring bread with some cheese, and a bottle of French wine that he kept for a special occasion, for which the lady was left looking somewhat puzzled because she did not know yet who that young woman was. For she asked the priest if he was sure of that. Well, she knew that the father kept that bottle with great zeal.

"This is a special occasion, a blessing from heaven, a miracle," Father Joaquin said. "Go on. No buts, Petra," the father insisted.

The lady left immediately along with Mama Chayo and the children to give them something to eat in the kitchen. Chendo had sat on one of the benches of the chapel. Philip entered with Elida and the priest into the sacristy so that Elida would tell him what had happened to her. Elida told Father Joaquin about how her stepfather had tried to kill her to keep her mother's life insurance, and her life insurance too, forcing her to sign some papers. By not agreeing with what he demanded of her, he hit her on the head knocking her unconscious. She was sure that he had been the culprit of her mother's death, so he could keep the life insurance money. That scoundrel had then tried to do the same with her, but for his wretched luck, he had not succeeded.

Elida's mother had died falling off the roof of a kindergarten where she was teaching, without anyone witnessing how chance had been, well only the director of the kindergarten was on the spot. The same she had married after being widowed from Elida's father, who had tried to kill her.

Elida's parents had met in the law school at the university of the city where they were living, and at the same time graduated from their specialty, in a short time they decided to marry. Well, love had shaken their feelings, as it does with everyone. Being Elida is the fruit of their love.

Her mother had worked in the kindergarten for more than ten years, in which she always worried about the service of others, that her parents had taught her since she was a child. She always got something to eat for the school kids because she said that a full belly was an open mind. Also, she got shoes and clothes for the children, sacrificing many times what she had to give to them.

Sometimes she organized classroom meetings to talk to parents about how important homeschooling, hygiene, and proper feeding is for children. Just like Grandma, she taught women about personal health, giving them things and medications, or what they needed most. Above all, she gave them advice on how important mutual respect was at home. That, in case of abuse they should trust their friends, so they would not allow any of them to be damaged because they did not want to report the person who could make them suffer. She always emphasized how important homeschooling was to children because they would reflect those values in their interaction with others outside the home. She spends hours visiting many of the children's homes, especially those in need, or who had any sign of child abuse.

On one occasion, she spends days attending the home of a family who had lost respect for the figure of the mother. Thanks to the degradation and mistreatment from the husband, the children learned what their father did when they were young. To the extent of becoming familiar with the mistreatment that the mother received daily from that poor ignorant, who did not know how to deal with himself because he was dependent on his wife for everything he needed. He could not do it himself, and he could not even serve the water on the table while she prepared the food. She always had to be the one to do all the work of cleaning and serving the table, as well such as washing clothes and ironing them to the husband's liking so that they would not see him badly dressed when he went to brag with friends, or that people would not see him badly when walking down the street.

Elida's mother had realized that the lady never attended the meetings she held every two weeks for the parents. At every meeting, she asked the other mothers about the lady, but none gave her a reason for what her life was like or why she was never attending meetings. Only in the morning, she got to see her when she left the child at the door of the kindergarten and often left him in the corner. She found it very strange that she did not want to approach and thought that there should be some reason for the lady's shyness. That is why she always insisted that the other ladies say something to her, but they always kept quiet.

One day she tried to stop her calling her to come back and talk to her about the child, as a pretext to find out what was wrong with her. She even yelled at her to stop for a minute, but the lady came out very hurriedly covering her face without stopping or turning to look back. That is when she decided to ask one of the ladies who were there, and that, besides she lives along the course of which the lady lived, to tell her the truth. Insisting on how important was for the lady's health, that women should support each other. The young woman agreed to tell her some things that were obvious in that neighborhood because everyone knew how rude the children were to the mother. No matter where they were, they always spoke to her without any consideration or respect, and even rudeness shouted at her in the street if she did not agree with what the children demanded of her at the time.

The same figure of the father was what the little ones wanted to imitate because that was the example they received since they were born, a cruel and unjust world lacking in love and affection.

That same day in the afternoon, she went to find that poor woman along with two municipal officers who agreed to accompany her after hearing the arguments she had to report the abuser. The officers already knew something about it, but they could not do anything without a lawsuit from the victim, as they had great respect for the teacher, they went with her to find out the truth once and for all.

When she opened the door, the lady was frightened to see the teacher with the two officers, who immediately tried to close it, but the officers prevented her. In that, Elida's mother came in and hugged her telling her that she understood her, that she would help her with everything she needed. The lady did not take long for her to feel the affection, that she for many years did not have from her family, in the sincere embrace of the teacher, she let go of the crying, begging her to take her away so they would not hurt her anymore.

She took her home for a while, where she learned the affection that children inherit from their parents by the example of mutual respect and service to others as they taught Elida. It was thanks to that environment that her spirit was filled with unmeasured goodness for their charity and service to others.

It was thanks to the support of Elida and her mother that, that woman regained love for her children, deciding to return for them and save them from the bitterness where they were because the husband had taken them to a hut that he had away from the village so that they would not be taken away. But the officers found him and took the children from him. Not without having to tie him by the hands before because he had fought with them with punches and bangs.

Elida's parents managed to get others to join the cause for that family, getting them a place to live, along with some furniture, clothes, and shoes with which some of the neighbors cooperated with great joy. One of the neighbors offered her work at his home to help him in the kitchen, for which the lady responded with great joy bathed in tears full of gratitude and blessings to all, for how generous they were to them. She felt the force that exerted the power of good in their hearts by offering them the opportunity to begin a new life.

Elida accompanied her parents every weekend to community service in the village parish where the kindergarten was. On her vacations from school, she went with her mother to help her with summer activities, until she graduated from high school to attend the same college her parents had attended.

Elida's father had died when she was sixteen, in the capital of the country, at the hands of the military police, at a student protest that spread socialism, freedom, and equanimity of goods and services for alike.

Governments do not like the socialist ideal with which new generations use to demand social justice and respect, they like capitalism, the beast of power. Being the blood that nourishes its branches, the monetary value over the aspirations that we decide to take in life, according to the model that has been implanted to participate deliberately.

Many of the things Elida talked about her past, Philip sensed that she was telling him. Well, the priest being her uncle was supposed to know something about the story. Father Joaquin held her hands as she looked at Philip who cried for what she told them.

"How did that villain come into your lives, what he did do with Josefa?" Father Joaquin asked her.

Elida said that two years after her father died and her mother had decided to marry the kindergarten director, she had decided to leave the house because of bad encounters she had had with her mother's new husband. Because on some occasions, he had come to sexually harass her when they were alone in the house, that is why she decided to leave. Before she departs, she accused him of her mother, and she believed her knowing that in her heart there was no lie, even though at one point she doubts to think that it was some frustration over her father's death. Somehow, she did not want anyone to impersonate him.

The mother's heart recognizes the truth in her children, listening to them carefully, with patience for their hearts to open with sincerity, trust, and respect.

Relying blindly on her daughter, faced her husband at that very moment.

The abuser ran away when he saw the decision of determination that Josefa had made, telling him that she would denounce him for the lowness he had committed, and for how miserable he was. That she did not hate him, but she hoped he would receive the punishment he deserved.

Josefa had not reported her husband's harassment to the authorities believing that he would disappear from their lives after that, even though Elida insisted that she do so. She better have had to leave the house because she thought maybe her mother wanted to go back with him, or something.

After a few months of starting her career as an agronomist at the country's autonomous university, Elida received the news that her mother had died. Feeling that the world was ending at that moment, that her life lost all meaning and courage in things because of the pain her heart suffered from having lost a piece of her soul. But it was worst than her pain to find out she had been buried a week earlier.

She immediately returned to the city to find out what had happened to her mother because she did not understand how such misfortune had passed, how was that she had fallen from the roof of the kindergarten.

As soon as she got there, she wanted to go see where her mother was buried. In that, the stepfather arrived very serenely without showing any feeling. Elida felt something suspicious about him, asking him immediately why he dared to show up at the time, well she sensed that that scoundrel had to do with all that.

The stepfather only told her that he was carrying some papers for her to sign, but she ignored him going to fetch her mother's grave. Some neighbors saw her in tears leaving the house, immediately offering her her condolences and asking her to come with them because all the neighbors had agreed to fix her mother's grave, as the stepfather had buried her very quickly and without warning.

Friends and neighbors joined Elida in prayers for Josefa, the teacher who dedicated her life to children and the community, serving and seeking justice for those most in need.

Upon returning home, Elida found the stepfather inside. As soon as he saw her, got up from where he was sitting demanding that she sign some papers about the funeral expenses, according to him. But Elida refused to sign, causing the stepfather's fury, who threatened her to sign. He took her by the hair and pushed her on the table where the papers were, gave her a pen to sign by yelling at her to do it or he would kill her too.

Elida's heart was coming in pain when she heard that the wretched man had killed her mother, that took strength from somewhere and let go of the claws of that beast, and she tried to flee to warn the authorities. But, as she tried to leave, she felt a blow to the back of her head that knocked her unconscious, and did not wake up long after near the dump. That wretch had tried to get rid of her after giving her up for dead in the dump.

Father Joaquin told them that after two months of her disappearing without a trace of what had happened to her, the neighbors sought help from the priest of the local church to locate Josefa's relatives. Being the same priest who informed Father Joaquin about the death of his sister and the disappearance of his niece.

The heart was broken from pain to Father Joaquin, to the degree of denying against the designs of the high, for all the mortal innocents that we must endure pain, the suffering, and the grief of losing those we love.

To inform his mother about the death of her daughter and the disappearance of her granddaughter, was in some way his due, not because he is a priest, but because he is her son.

Grandma almost died of a heart attack upon learning of the news, that Father Joaquin had to help her to wake up, along with the butler and the lady of the kitchen, who immediately brought a couple of aspirins with some water. A sea of tears formed the pain of misfortune, that all who always accompanied her were joined in a great embrace around her; so, as a family suffers together that painful loss of those they loved.

Grandma asked Father Joaquin to immediately take her to the place where such misfortune had occurred, to find out what had really happened. She wanted to know more than Father Joaquin had told her because was obvious that there were many irregularities and coincidences that made her suspect what Father Joaquin had already intuited, from the moment that the priest of the chapel of the village where the kindergarten was located, had told him about the details, along with what the neighbors had told him about Elida's stepfather.

They went to the house that Elida's father had built with his own hands, in which they lived many birthdays together, and some other Christmas when Grandma visited them. Because in some years, they were dedicated to handing out food through the houses of low-income families that they did not have to celebrate at that special moment. On Christmas Grandma visited them, and she would go with them to bring things to give to the people she held so dear.

The neighbors, upon recognizing her, approached her immediately to offer their condolences and tell her what they had seen about Elida's stepfather. They had seen him come out in a hurry the same day Elida was around, but had not seen Elida come out, they had only seen her come in.

The next morning, they were made suspicious not to see Elida come out all day. Already in the afternoon, they decided to go knock on the door to bring her something to eat and be with her for a while so she would not feel alone. They approached trying to knock but found the door semi-open, so they called her repeatedly, without any answer. It was then that they decided to go in and see if anything had happened to Elida.

They found no sign of her anywhere, and it looked like she had not taken her things because they were on top of the bed half packed, for which they decided immediately to warn the authorities of what they suspected.

Grandma met with the district judge who had taken the case to see if she could find anything to guide her to her granddaughter's whereabouts, and what had happened to her daughter. The judge told her that the stepfather had disappeared after collecting Josefa's life insurance. That, in the interrogation, he had asked him about Elida, and this individual told him that she had already gone back to college and that she had ceded all insurance rights to him. He had submitted all the documentation in order to collect the insurance. He also told her that the insurance agent was present with his lawyer for the signing of the check.

The judge had asked him not to leave town as the investigations of his wife's death continued; for so he told him that he had no more reason to stay there, but that he would stay to show that he had nothing to fear. That same day he ran away in the afternoon.

Trying not to let nobody see him leave, left his car several blocks from the house to get out by the backdoor, without bringing anything with him more than his cowardice.

The grandmother, having heard what the judge informed her about the facts, was dissatisfied with the service that the judiciary exercises in enforcing the law and justice. That is why she decided to take the search for her granddaughter on her own, hiring private investigators to look for Elida's whereabouts, and at the same time, they will look for the bastard who had fled cowardly.

Arriving at the village where the kindergarten was, Grandma and Father Joaquin went straight to the village chapel to speak to the priest, who informed them of the same facts people said. They stayed only for a few minutes just because the chapel was on road to the cemetery, well they immediately went straight to Josefa's grave.

They brought with them her favorite pack, which was a bag made of maguey pita, that she always used as a child to bring things to her friends when she went on community service with her parents, and the same she always carried in her whole life to the kindergarten with food for her students.

Many people approached Grandma to offer their condolences, with a certain mixed feeling for the pleasure of seeing her and the penalty of her daughter's death. Either way, people had formed a great respect for the teacher Josefa, who had formed a commemorative plaque for her to put in her grave, but they were waiting for a relative to arrive to ask for their permission.

Grandma realized how much people loved and respected her, seeing how they had adorned the commemorative plaque. But the pain in her chest made her lose her will, which made her kneel before her daughter's grave.

Yes, it is true she felt dying, and she wants to, but also felt a big pride in her spirit, which made her feel great respect for the noble work that Josefa had done every day of her life.

Grandma got up with the help of some old friends from the village who loved her very much since they were teenagers. Thanking them and embracing many when recognizing them. Feeling a great pride seeing so many young men almost made, who had helped for many years, and seeing that they had become good young men.

Grandma was pleased by the work her daughter had continued after her. After all, served the great example she always gave her with the service and goodwill with which she shared.

Suddenly joy came to many, motivated by Father Joaquin and Father Gerardo, with the argument that Josefa would not have liked them to suffer grief.

Despite feeling the pain of her loss, they said that she would like to see them happy, just as she always wanted. Suddenly everyone began to sing praises and songs to her, the same ones she had taught them in the church choir.

Saying goodbye to who had taught them so much in their lives, they savored a little jubilation around the tomb of teacher Josefa, just because Grandma accompanied them with a couple of songs to honor the great work her daughter had done with the people of that village, who loved her so much as to say goodbye to her singing the praises she had taught them.

At that time, Elida embraced Father Joaquin with a great feeling after hearing how the people had honored her mother, with so much affection and respect for the work she had done for them every day of her life.

Philip was proud to hear how Father Joaquin told them what had happened that afternoon around the grave of Elida's mother, teacher Josefa. Out of the respect that people had taken for her selfless service, and the way she had been honored with the commemorative plaque for her work. Thanks to the great honorable dedication her parents had instilled in her since she was a child, they tried to do until her death.

"We must warn Grandma, she must know that you are still alive," Father Joaquin very excitedly told to Elida.

Elida insisted that he should say nothing because she feared that her mother's killer would try to hurt her grandmother too. Father Joaquin insisted on her by telling her that he would do it in the most discreet way possible, that she should trust him.

He told them that he was about to leave for the state archdiocese to report to the bishop and that after meeting with him, he would take the opportunity to go to see his mother and inform her about the miracle that had happened.

Father Joaquin promised to return in a couple of weeks to take them with Grandma, which Philip found somewhat awkward to think that he would go with them to Grandma's house.

He felt something alienated from the life Elida had, but he loved her so much that he was willing to protect her with his own life, for he did not doubt the possibility of leaving the dump if it was necessary. He remembered that the stepfather wanted to kill her, and he stared at Elida's belly and her seven months of pregnancy, feeling the need to take them back.

At that moment Philip rose from the chair a little anxious without knowing what to say.

Father Joaquin realized his discomfort when he saw him worrying, pulling the dirt out of his fingernails, of the anxiety caused by uncertainty about what might happen to his loved ones in the future.

Somehow, the priest understood, for he felt Philip's concern for not knowing how to protect his family. Father Joaquin suggested that he feared nothing because God would protect his own at any time and everywhere.

That, if necessary, they could stay in the parish the time he returned from his task. Philip stared into his eyes telling him that he would take care of their safety, that they would be safer at the dump because no one could ever find them there. The priest seemed pleased.

Elida, hearing what Philip had said, stood from the chair and walked towards him, took him by the arm, and leaned on his shoulder. Father Joaquin looked at them with a big smile and stood immediately to give them a hug, telling them that God had united them with a purpose and that they would never let anything separate them.

Mrs. Petra, interrupted at the time telling them it was time to eat, to move into the kitchen.

Father Joaquin was absent for a while, while they were eating to prepare the things he should take for the trip to the archdiocese. He returned on time when they finished eating, to take Elida for a little walk in the parish garden, well Father Joaquin had not told her some things that her grandmother had done with the village kindergarten

Felipe stayed in the kitchen with Chendo, Mama Chayo, and the children, under the care of the sacristan who suggested to them every time if they liked to go and pray for a moment. After a while, Mama Chayo attended to him in one of his so many insistences, so he did not feel that he was despised, taking Chendo and the children with them.

While he was still at the table looking at the window that faced the garden where an endless of flowers of all kinds and colors grew, he felt a strange sensation that made him want to return to the sacristy. Philip started checking his stuff to see if he had forgotten anything, but everything in his backpack seemed to be in place.

He did not understand the nature of such a feeling that insisted on his thinking, nor why he felt the need to return to the sacristy; but, as he saw through the window Elida and Father Joaquin walking in the garden, he had a sudden glimpse of a man with a book in his hands, resembling the one he had seen on one of his visions.

Philip took advantage of the moment when everyone was busy doing something and immediately went to the sacristy to satisfy a little curiosity, about what might be calling his attention. Philip got in without showing not wanting to be seen, but in a very respectful way up to Father Joaquin's desk. He stood looking at the desk for a few seconds, feeling a big lump in his throat and a pressure on his chest that made him bend a little. He had to lean with one hand on the desk so as not to fall to the ground. And at that moment, he felt a shiver above his head that ran down his neck up to the height of his shoulders, being able to clearly see the book inside Father Joaquin's desk.

Mrs. Petra entered precisely as Philip was about to fall to the ground, and rushed right away to help him, avoiding that he hit his head with the chair he was sitting in when they talked to the father Joaquin about what had happened after Elida had disappeared.

As she could, sat him in the chair until he was able to regain his lucidity and gave him some of the wine father Joaquin had on the desk, to pass the lump in his throat.

Philip took the glass with trembling hands even with the desire to cry, drinking a couple of drinks of that wine that made him completely regain the lucidity in this reality.

"Some say, somehow your destiny calls you," said Mrs. Petra, as she poured him a little more wine in the glass.

She took him back to the kitchen without giving him any explanation, but without asking him anything that had happened to him. She gave him some bread and cheese to have with the wine. Philip took it and savored it cordially, that at that moment he forgot all indication of awareness about this reality, letting himself be carried away by the taste of bread and cheese that became in Mana when passing it with the wine.

Somehow, he understood after regaining his conscience, that he had to shut up what had happened to him in the sacristy because he was not sure yet of what fate was trying to show him with its sudden hints.

"Diligently Philip, diligently," Mrs. Petra said while she was fixing more bread and cheese to be taken on their way back to the dump.

Later, several people from the village gathered to say goodbye to Father Joaquin on his way to the state archdiocese. Chendo and Philip, along with the sacristan, helped get things up from the father to the truck that would take him to the nearest city, then take a plane to the state capital. Mrs. Petra had given him a little bag with something to eat for the road, the same thing she had given Philip, which Father Joaquin took with him as he got in the truck so he can taste it after he was attacked by hunger.

As the truck that would take Father Joaquin to the city drives away, they decided to return as soon as possible to their huts in the dump.

While the sacristan and Chendo enlisted the details of the return, Philip stood next to Elida to say goodbye to Father Joaquin in his commitment. Together with them was Mrs. Petra taking Elida by the hand.

The sacristan helped Chendo with the mule to put it in the wagon, along with the oldest of the children who was always on the lookout to learn. For they had taken the poor beast out of the wagon to rest when they had just arrived at the chapel. Mrs. Petra, saying goodbye to Elida gave her a blessing on her chest and on her belly, praying in a language she had never heard. Elida thought that was the lady's native language, so she did not ask about what she was saying, believing in her heart that whatever she told her was a good thing for them, that she had nothing to fear.

They boarded the wagon very happy and immediately headed back home.

As they passed the corner, they realized that the two elders who had received them with reverence when they arrived, were bowing as they passed back to where the elders were, that everyone returned the same reverence with their heads as a sign of respect.

At that moment, Philip thought of the clues that fate shows in our way, so that we may realize the importance of the lesson that will help us grow more as spirits, rebelling a little at a time about the mystery that envelops the veil of reason.

Philip remembered the words of The Old Lady with the White Hair, about the fate which himself had agreed to carry out the mission that The Purest had entrusted to him, to help his brothers in the carnal life; to prepare as much as they could while they were in the body, to transcend worthily closer to Him on the path of purification.

Philip accepted what he understood until then, of what God had entrusted to him, but he was still somewhat concerned about how he would do so that everyone could somehow hear what he would have to tell them because he was a beggar who lived in a dump, poorly dressed and unconcerned with how his unkept hair looked, which allowed himself to grow in each winter. Sometimes he would let it grow into summer, saying it was because the hair was a kind of antenna that made him pick up vibrations of energies that people very often ignore in their daily lives.

The Way Back

At first, no one dared say anything because everyone followed the sea of their thinking privately, that they could only hear the worn ball bearings from the wagon and the footsteps of the mule when walking.

The children broke the ice by beginning to discuss issues that most people find uncomfortable, or at least they try to evade with ego and vanity by losing faith in what goes beyond this reality.

Thoughts go, thoughts came, thus many more will come that will keep us busy for a while until we free ourselves from the bonds that bind us to the body, so let us continue the path we have chosen since before we were born in this flesh.

The little ones were arguing about death and what was possible after it. The elders only listened to the innocence with which the little ones dealt with the subject, without considering the vicissitudes that life would present to them as they grew up; so, they only listened to them without interrupting those witty talks that children used to have very often.

Philip felt within his heart the difference between the good and the bad that exists in the world. At all times he devoted himself to doing good to every being who required his sincere and noble help.

He knew he could not help everyone, therefore when he learned of some misfortune that happened to others far from where he could have helped them, Philip wished with all his heart that someone would help them with a little peace and hope. He always wished with all his heart that everyone would be fine in the area where the catastrophe had occurred, but he felt guilty that he could not go and help them because he did not have the necessary means.

Perhaps, we all should do an introspection within ourselves, to discern why we do not take sides to help those who need it, by the reason that everyone accepts the reunion with your truth.

It was those occasions when he failed, which made him feel that he was not yet prepared to counter the pride, vanity, and temptation that are poured into his weaknesses as an earthly man, on every branch that uses this beautiful psycho-biological bridge that life has formed so that the spirit can influence matter.

Lost in these thoughts, Philip did not ignore the discussion of the little ones who talked about how the body took life when it was born; by which, the youngest said, "Since before, I believe."

The children turned to see their dad and see if he had anything to say. Chendo very serenely pointed to Philip without saying anything, he just turned to see him, and the children turned to see Philip too, who nodded that the little one had some reason in the innocent words with which he had referred to the arrival of the spirit to the body before being born.

"But it is a mystery that everyone must discover for themselves," he told them. "Do not forget to learn as much as you can." The children were pleased with Philip's words, for one could see the pride with which the little one smiled, at the knowledge that what he had said was somewhat right. Without no idea what life had prepared for him on the way that he should discover on his own, without someone else approving or disapproving of his opinion of the truth. Well, only his truth can discover, then will know that it is a single truth for all spirits without exception.

Elida and Mama Chayo planned in the back of the wagon what they were going to do during the week, ignoring the talks of others. While the children were behind Chendo, Philip, and the older boy who was sitting in the middle of the two in front of the wagon, so he can hear the stories they were talking about and not get bored on the way back to the dump.

Being close to arrival, they were able to appreciate the amber of the sunset over the clouds, as everyone turned now when the little one warned them about that beautiful sunset, illuminating with that magical light their faces. They boasted of being able to appreciate a

such beautiful sunset. In addition, they felt the arrival of the freshness of the afternoon, that as the light, hit on their pleased faces
with the gift that the creator had squandered before them without
discrimination.

The night took to remove the colors of things the time it took
them to get to the dump, untie the mule from the wagon and lower
the half-filled bags of the food that Mrs. Petra had given them for
the road. Mama Chayo and the children entered with Elida to her
hut for a while, while they finished putting the mule into Chendo's
corral.

Philip sought answers among the clouds that were fading when
the queen of dreams covered them with her etheric mantle, waiting
for a sign to tell him the best thing he needed to do to protect his
family. Not only of the world and its prejudices but of the evil with
which men have polluted to the degree of murder by zeal or greed.

Philip was at the end of the day with new fears and anguish to
dream, wondering how it was possible for the good ones to always
suffer and the tyrants would get away with it in most cases.

Standing on a pile of rubbish looking at the last vestiges of the
light of that day, understood the responsibility of protecting his family, that was the most useful thing he had discovered until then to do
in life. The message that was deciphered in Elida's pregnancy made
him feel the strength and the decision that he would never stop at
anything or anyone, to ensure a better world for them, even knowing
that his dreams were impossible to realize in this world. He felt in his
heart that his destiny would take him to where no man ever imagined, well he had seen it before in a dream, but he did not remember
because he was still very small when he had that revelation, which
had been deliberately diluted into the luminous dust of his dreams,
for some reason he was willing to discover.

"Why so much pain, no one cares?" Philip thought before he got
down off the garbage heap to head to his hut.

Not even saying goodbye to Chendo, who could see Philip that
he almost got lost in the dark. Just because the light of the lamp
oil of his hut came out through one of the holes illuminating him
on the path. Chendo shouted to him to warn his wife to bring the

children to prepare them dinner. For which Philip mocked him telling him it was only a pretext because he wanted to dine. Chendo answered asking him to do it because it was time for the children to go to bed.

Chapter 7
The Dream Design and the Pectoral

The next morning, he was noticed with dark circles for not being able to sleep properly throughout the night, due to the visions he had during the time lapses he fell asleep thinking over and over about what to do to ensure the well-being of his family.

Elida prepared him something to eat as usual and put it in his backpack along with some water in his cantina. Noticed a concern in his gaze, and she immediately approached him to hug him. Philip hugged her a little more than usual very hard against his chest.

"I love you, skinny," Philip told her.

She told him to not worry, that she would be fine and that he should not neglect the work because they would need resources to carry out the plans they had formed together.

Philip armed himself with courage thinking that they would soon be a family of three and that he should strive to seek better opportunities for the new innocent being who came into the world, so that would not suffer the same fate he had had in his life.

He met with the others on the side of the dump, who noticed his distraction, but nobody said a single word to not be distracted from his worries.

The new morning illuminated a little the reason, on that subliminal sea of thought, while they wait for Uicho to pick them up with Zorro to take them to work at the construction site.

Philip was very quiet and thoughtful when young Raziel said to him:

"You must prepare your heart, to abandon everything."

"Hey, my dear, don't sting this fool with that," Chendo begged Raziel.

The other young man named Gabriel, let out a laugh along with Chendo at the same time. Then he took him near the eucalyptus tree, leaving Raziel and Philip alone so they could talk. Chendo went with him without even realizing the real intention, he just kept laughing very happy talking to Gabriel about the branches of the eucalyptus, wondering how its flowers looked, while Philip listened to the advice of that mysterious young man.

The mind navigates among this sea of thought, in a flow that does not let us hear the inner voice which warns us about the details that we do not commonly appreciate, losing the opportunity that such details could reveal on the way to each one.

All this mystery that unfolded in his thought on the way to the work, about the advice of young Gabriel, the unreal of The Old Lady with the White Hair, and the obligation to protect his family from Elida's evil stepfather; also, from the injustice that was in the world, were the indications that fate was sneaking into that immense sea that kept him deliberately occupied.

"Serenity is a good example of strength when it comes to fighting back the tide in thinking," Gabriel told him, while Philip tried to see the Old Lady's house as they entered the streets of the village.

Then he leaned on The Zorro folds, trying to find some peace in the storm of his concerns. At work, he was limited only to one yes or no to the questions Chendo asked him while working on the facade of the central building. Chendo had to ask him what was wrong with him but knowing him well, he thought it was one of those ailments that he sometimes had, and he did not ask him anymore.

When lunchtime came Philip almost ran out to go see if he could find any answers or advice with The Old Lady with the White Hair because he was sure she would know what was going on and she could give him the help he needed to cope with the helplessness he felt when the world let him down.

Philip arrived faster than usual after having almost run to the house, and he had to stop for a few seconds at the entrance to take some air. He heard the sublime voice of the old woman, who reminded him of the words of young Raziel and immediately entered as far as the Old Lady was sitting on the bluestone and sat in front of her.

"A great fortune you would receive for the jewel you bring on your neck," the Old Lady told him, as she walked to a corner where she had many strange things that Philip could not recognize.

"Fortune? Wealth disturbs the heart of man with injustices," Philip said.

Philip was wearing the medallion; he had worn it for a few days because of a feeling he had when he woke up one day.

The Old Lady interrupted him by giving him a bowl with something she had prepared for him and asked him to drink a little. Philip took it a little indecisively. She asked him to close his eyes the moment he took a sip of the bowl.

"What do you want most in life?" the Old Lady asked him, now she pointed the spear at the medallion.

Without opening his eyes, Philip answered:

"Impossible." Then he kept quiet for a few seconds thinking of the souls that had been lost in the flood.

"Are you afraid the same thing will happen?" the Old Lady asked him because Philip was distressed to think that he might lose those he loved because of the foolish and indifference to justice.

"Men don't understand, they don't listen. No way to rid them of greed for power and money," answered Philip some mad.

The Old Lady asked him to drink some more. Philip took his second sip while the Old Lady asked him:

"Why do you want to save them all, if many are evil, they would never do anything for you, nor for anyone?"

"There are some good ones," Philip answered her. "People like Elida and her family, the saint, you and me." The Old Lady revealed to him what was happening with The Tools of Order, well throughout the different ages, since men had been created in this world, there had been means to help them in their reunion with the truth. The one that is lost by the veil in the coming to carnal life. She warned him that men are distracted by other vicissitudes that are not of great help to the spirit, nor to their lives in the material world.

Somehow, he had already realized the existence of these tools, that helped the man defend the individuality of his being, to transcend in the hope he assimilated into his heart, but which very few dared to discover within themselves.

"What should I do to warn them?" asked Philip, right after having meditated for a few seconds on what the Old Lady said.

"Is there anything you need to do?"

"I don't know. Everyone talks about helping the poor, but very few do anything," Philip said while the Old Lady asked him to drink a little more from the bowl.

Taking the third sip, Philip stood thinking very seriously about what he could do, as well as what he could not change in others. He knew that he could influence those closest to him, by the example he always gave them with his good deeds.

"What can you do?" the Old Lady asked him, as Philip opened his eyes.

"If I don't change, no one would listen to me." The Old Lady removed the spear from the medallion, and Philip sat for a moment in front of her, with his head down thinking of the villain who wanted to take his family's life. The greedy wanted to disappear Elida to collect the life insurance with the papers that credited him as the only beneficiary, which had made her sign by force when he had tried to kill her.

Philip had already realized that Elida's family was of a social level totally opposite to where she lived with him in the hut, and he worried that she would want to reclaim her position by wanting to return to her grandmother to be more comfortable with better services. He felt helpless at what her family might offer her, and he feared she would abandon him. But then regained his reason thinking that he should not get carried away by that because she loved him enough, well she felt that she was with him because she loved him not because she wanted to run away from her stepfather.

Philip stood up, returning the bowl to the Old Lady, he looked into her eyes and told her he would come back later when needed.

"The key is in your heart," the Old Lady told him, as Philip was about to leave the place.

He kept thinking a little about what the Old Lady had told him because it seemed very familiar to him, but which he had not yet fully understood. In the rush to return to the construction site, he lost the thread of his reasoning with new thoughts, which were related to what he had to live at work.

A little more focused, Philip arrived to talk to Chendo about some techniques that he had learned in the books, to apply them to the facade of the house so that they could finish sooner. Chendo, knowing him well, went with the flow when he realizes that it was a good idea, and they immediately began to work on it.

After a while, Philip felt a strange feeling that made him think of Uicho, so he asked Chendo if he knew where Uicho was. Chendo told him that he was in the office since they had gone to eat, that he had not left at all.

"What the, if he never spends it there," Philip said.

"Well, who knows," Chendo said.

Philip listened to his intuition and went to find Uicho, who was in the small back room of the building, which they used to save the tools, as the blueprint for the construction site. He carried his backpack with him because he kept in it the design he had made, hoping that the foreman could look at it.

Uicho was looking at the blueprint now Philip walked in because the door had opened as soon as Philip had touched it. He slowly entered where Uicho was trying to find a way to fix the irregularities of the blueprint as best he could to not do something that would then fall off. Uicho turned to see right away when he felt that someone had come in.

"What do you think we can do?" Uicho asked him.

"Maybe I can help you, but at the end of the day you're the boss," Philip insisted staring him in the eye. "The decision will be yours whether we do it or not."Philip got the blueprint out of his bag pack and gave it to Uicho, who took it somewhat surprised that Philip gave him a clean and error-free blueprint, that he stayed checking it out for a while. It was the first time in his life, in he got the chance to appreciate such harmony with which that design was made, which made him feel a different joy, well he worked on all kinds of buildings with different styles, but none like the style Philip had used in his design.

Philip was convinced of the visions he had had regarding that part of his life because he knew that things would be given in a certain way so that, that design he had made in the hut would come true.

Philip felt his heart rate accelerate by corroborating how the visions materialized, for which he began to sweat all over his body and feel chills that made him tremble without control.

Uicho asked him to leave him alone to think seriously about what he would decide to make about the changes he suggested. Philip knew that Uicho would not risk his reputation by building things that would collapse later. He was sure that no sensible man would deny that he was right about the mistakes of the previous design, and this time it was no exception. Well, Uicho recognized the talent that Philip had in having designed the entrance and the facade of the construction, being a poor beggar who lived in the dump. Uicho seriously thought of applying it in the work, as revenge on the engineer who had degraded and mistreated him in all those years in which he worked for him. For this reason, Uicho planned to take seriously that beggar ignored by the world and carry out the design he had made for the entrance of the construction, in addition to a few tweaks to the facade of the buildings so that it would be assimilated to the style of the entrance with the pillars.

Uicho spends the entire afternoon observing the details that Philip had drawn. He did not remember having built something that resembled such a design, with so little material to use. It looked like something very practical and simple for him. He liked it so much that he felt in his heart a joy that he had not felt before in any of the works he worked for the engineer, well none had the simplicity and beauty like the one Philip had made. He was willing to make that design to prove to the engineer that he was wrong by judging others by their appearance or social position. He was not afraid of him anymore.

Mounted on The Zorro back to the dump and almost leaving the village, Philip thought to ask the Saint about social justice and the rights that every man should have by nature, among other things.

"Man has the right to love. But the right for goods and services, which are pursued in the model that society has formed, is linked to material attachment," the Saint explained to him. "Well, man being poor or rich, will experience the same vicissitudes in life as everyone else, but only in the individual nature of his spirit, the details of his lesson will be given in carnal life."

Philip kept thinking seriously about what the Saint was trying to explain to him, but he continued with a certain dissatisfaction about the treatment that many poor people received from the society that they themselves fed with their work.

"Do the poor have no right to the basic goods and services in society?" Philip asked him a little disappointed.

The Saint stared into his eyes, put his right hand on his shoulder, and spoke.

"They chose their part by approving the covenant they pleased agreed to be part of the representation of their names before society. When we get rid of all that, even from our own name, which we have been given at birth in this life, then we will begin the path to freedom of the spirit, which we will conclude in the separation of the body when we die." It was clear the determination in the Saint, without any greed for the material, for which Philip was filled with pride and great satisfaction. Above all, to have his advice, at least when it was possible for him to attend Philip because he was always in different places dealing with matters necessary for his spiritual journey.

At work, the Saint always asked for all those who worked there, for their family and friends when he blessed the food. You never heard him as for something for himself. On the contrary, he took the bread out of his mouth to give it to another when they shared food at mealtime, and he was always willing to help anyone who asked for a hand in the work. He knew them all by name and asked them about their children or relatives when it was his turn to be near them, that everyone had a very special respect for the humility of heart with which he addressed his words of encouragement all the time, to try to soften any discomfort that living was causing them.

Oddly enough, Chendo did not seem to hear what they had been talking about all the way back, for he was looking lost in some dream that some rare reason worked on him so that he was not part of the message that Philip received from the Saint. Gabriel and Raziel were bowing with their heads at the same time they clasped their hands, now when the Saint responded to the concerns with which Philip insisted on him.

Philip no longer thought it was anything strange. "We are just passing through Philip," Raziel said, as he reached out his hand pointing at Gabriel, who was sitting in the center of the truck in the lotus flower position, behind the cockpit. Raziel, next to where the Saint and Philip were.

Gabriel nodded now that Philip turned to see him, in a sign of approval regarding what had been said, just at the time when the Saint and Raziel pointed their hand at him in the same way.

The Saint was one of the pillars in Philip's life, as far as the spirit is concerned, well he was always at the times he needed him to seek his advice.

Philip thought of Elida and the baby that they would soon have, as an impossible reason to ignore when making any decision to abandon everything, if it was necessary for his personal lesson for which he resisted that it was the only way to transcend.

In a way, the idea of leaving the world and its distractions was always his philosophy. After Elida's arrival and her pregnancy, it was that he changed the way he perceived the individuality of his being, and the obligations he should take to ensure a better future for those he loved.

"Saint, one cannot abandon those we love. It's our destiny," Philip told him.

"Few are capable among those chosen to carry out certain tasks in carnal life. Don't grit if your destiny is fulfilled as some have already happened," the Saint told him.

"Then, will everyone have their lesson according to their destiny, or mission that they must face in life?" Philip inquired.

"Everything has a motive, which is personal and intimate of the creator, and it will be revealed to each one according to the plan agreed by God in the carnal life; so, gradually in every step that leads to spiritual perfection. Being a need for each spirit, to find the reason that will help you grow," the Saint insisted. "No one could tell you what your heart feels or what your soul craves."Philip understood that the inner awakening was intimate to all men alike, that likewise, everyone had the potential to discern how to feed the energies necessary to achieve a balance, so as not to suffer the attachment for the offal that could manage to drop in their search for reason. That an institution was not necessary to mediate between the soul and the higher spirits because God in all his benevolence and wisdom, had created things in this way to teach us a personal lesson in the spirit, and that it would not be intelligible to man if they clung to material things, but which would be revealed within the self at the time necessary in life.

Even with a busy mind, Philip kept reasoning about some things he felt would give him some clue as to what his fate was trying to tell him. As The Zorro got lost in a cloud of dust, leaving the four of them at the banks of the dump, right in front of the eucalyptus tree that Raziel used to meditate in the evenings.

At Gabriel's suggestion, they agreed to meet at the back of Philip's hut, which was where he had his orchard of legumes and species, which Elida cared very jealously. Also, the hole he had made for the fish he had brought with him when they went hunting last time with the children.

Elida, Mama Chayo, and Inés, knowing that friends would come to hang out, each put in some of the little they had for the reunion.

Everything was filled with a party atmosphere and convivial, where they boasted very happy to see the children running and screaming all over the place, while adults talked about stories that life had taught them.

Fortunately, Philip's hut was far enough away from the central part of the dump, which was where the leaders lived. They never suspected the happiness with which they lived almost every day. Well, it became a custom to gather often in the evenings to share joy among them, despite they are living marginalized in misery. But only material because they were immensely fortunate by the nobility of their heart.

The irresistible call of the sunset with a living canvas full of amber light from the sun, as it hides between the three hills that crossed the horizon, illuminating that whole side of the dump, seducing Philip into accompanying it. Melancholy took hold of his memories to such an extent of almost crying for missing his parents that he had long lost.

He thought about the fortitude that his parents gave him during all those years of solitude, and all the occasions when he somehow disobeyed the advice, they gave him to pay attention to life.

He regretted making his mother cry over the rebellion that one day attacked him in his teens. And one day when he grew up, he realized that she was right in what she was trying to warn him about, but it was too late to remedy.

Without least appreciating the effort our parents could make in life to give us a better chance than they might have had, understanding that time passed for us too; understand their suffering and needs as individuals, so that we may enjoy their experiences respectfully and lovingly at every moment we have the privilege of being close to them, our parents in this world; And so, let us prepare in the best way for when we have to leave the body, without leaving any misunderstanding, so that the one who stays does not be a burden on the conscience.

Gabriel approached him slowly to enjoy with him the sunset. Raziel followed him as always beside him; at least when he did not entrust him with any diligence to carry some message.

Gabriel took him by the shoulder and say, "Philip, this will be passing for you, but it is good for them to remember them with love."

Philip embraced Gabriel crying like a heartbroken child feeling his words, which had reminded him of the offenses that in his eagerness for rebellion he had committed against whom he loved. And he understood that, despite having understood the lesson that his failures in life had taught him, he could not change what he had done.

"Calm Philip, the opportunity will be given to you in its time to clear up the misunderstandings with those who live in this world, then in the spiritual," Gabriel told him serenely, staring him in the eye.

Philip took strength from the good memories he had of them, enough to stop crying out of anguish and cry with joy at the living memory that came from his mother singing in the evenings while weaving some clothes to sell.

"She sang nice," Philip said, with a lump in his throat.

"We did not doubt it," Gabriel replied, pointing to Raziel and smiling a little.

"And you, do not you sing Philip?" Raziel asked him.

"My mother was the privileged one in that talent, I write," Philip replied.

"Of course," Gabriel and Raziel responded at the same time.

"When will you show us your cave?" Gabriel asked him.

Few things surprised him during these stays of his life, and he immediately offered to take them on Wednesday afternoon after returning from work because he spent Tuesday practicing with a piano he had found. Elida taught him how to play and read the musical notes every Tuesday afternoon, as they occupied the other days for different activities. And his piano lessons were more important than anything, which never for any reason let any class pass, well he was always punctual with perfect assistance.

That night, after saying goodbye to everyone and being left alone, Elida and Philip relied on how well they had had that afternoon of joy with their friends.

Moments that are left behind, and that we will only keep in our memories to identify with who we are, in the moments that we take hold of them, either by will, or because we have been influenced, suggested by some spirit with an interest that only that spirit knows, and which will be understood at the time by all men after material death.

Elida told Philip what Father Joaquin had told her about her grandmother, as they walked through the chapel garden. He told her that her grandmother had arranged the kindergarten where her mother had died. And that, for all the love the people of the village had for her, they had put the name Josefa Najera de Almaraz to the kindergarten, in memory of the teacher who had taught them by her example the good values she had learned from her parents. She always tried for everyone equally, during all that time she worked, and managed to bring respect and good manners back to the family bosom in many of the families of that village. Father Joaquin had told her that Grandma gave a grant to the village parish so that the children of the schools could have a decent breakfast, such as her daughter has tried for the ten years serving everyone in the village. Philip had enough to dream that night.

At work still thought about what Grandma had done with the schools of that village. He was afraid that Elida would want to return to Grandma to enjoy the comforts that money can buy.

At lunchtime, he went to find Uicho to find out what he had decided about the blueprint. Philip would like to know if Uicho was sensible enough to realize that the best solution was the design he had made. Although he was sure of himself, he felt a sense of uncertainty about how things would develop to achieve his goal. Uicho was very sure of himself, the moment Philip entered the room where they kept the work tools. Uicho had a smile from ear to ear that he could not contain when he saw Philip come in.

Tired of the abuses and degradations that the engineer made him, he had convinced himself to carry out such a great work that Philip had been designed with pieces of recycled paper from the rubbish. Because he would not jeopardize his reputation by building something that would collapse, well, then nobody would ever trust him again after that happened. The truth is that he was excited about Philip's design, well never in his years of experience had he had the opportunity to appreciate such simplicity and flexibility in any of the works he had succeeded in building. That is why he was determined no matter what consequences with the engineer because he no longer feared him, and he would face him if necessary.

Philip was well surprised when Uicho told him that they would build his design, that he embraced him tightly by telling him that it was the most sensible thing he could have done, that he would not regret it in the end.

"Calmly my poet," Uicho told him.

To Philip it seemed strange that he had called him that way; so Uicho continued to say after he realized that Philip had been surprised when he called him a poet, "The Chendo, you know how communicative he is. Don't worry, I like poetry too, I give it a look occasionally when there's time."

Uicho asked him not to tell anyone about what he had decided to do with the entry of the construction site so that the word would not spread, as almost always happens, and the engineer could get to know before they were done. He wanted to be sure that they would conclude their task within the two months that the engineer had already paid him in advance on his last visit to the site. He asked Philip to return to continue with the facade for this week, and that next week they would begin marking the area where the entrance would be built.

Feeling the pride inside his chest, Philip appreciated the world as if it were a different one from where he had lived all this time, when understood the importance of the work that our hands do, to satisfy the pride that is created within our aspirations. He did not think of profiting on the merit of his creation, he tried to take the attention so that he can send the message in a more subtle way, so they could hear him, by recognizing him as someone important.

All afternoon he was a joy which was overflowing on his smile. Very attentive and helpful with everyone.

Chendo, his great friend and godfather, noticed something that did not fit his personality, that is why he asked him:

"And what do you have then?"

"The premonitions of destiny, you know," Philip answered whit the usual mystery.

That was enough so Chendo would not ask him anymore because he knew what he was like, that he thought it was one more of his ailments of sanity that he suddenly had

On the way back to the dump, Philip spends thinking about the prestige he would gain after they would build his design, the possibilities he could use to offer Elida a better good to be, and that way she would not abandon him to go with her grandmother. No one crossed any words with him, seeing that his mind and countenance changed in a very remarkable way.

The same enthusiasm was reflected in Elida as he enters the hut, who immediately realized there was something different in him because he did not look as usual. That even his personality sounded different from how he approached any subject.

Among that pride spell, he told Elida that their lives would change in a way that no one could degrade them as beggars anymore. Elida, hearing him say arbitrariness, interrupted him with a kiss on his mouth to shut up and stop trying to be someone else. Philip, when he could not help others in a material way, in his heart desired well-being of all who needed more than just money to have a better life. But this time, his intention focused on a thought that had imprisoned him with the tentacles of its singularity, of its nature of profit and greed. Without realizing how he got to that point, the ego imprisoned him thinking about the prestige he could gain, and the money enough to be able to offer a dignified life for his family.

Surely, he misunderstood her because she did not feel the same that was torturing Philip's mind with his absurd fears because it had no basis on her part.

The unconditional love with which she treated him, caused him to yield to his aberration for wanting to conquer the world to build a castle for his queen: Which would be only a fortress of pride that would only serve as a cloister full of doubts, where they could not see the light of simplicity and humility if the shadow of greed took hold of him. In the end, Philip managed to regain lucidity by falling into the candor of Elida's fire belly, which made him feel as if his body was in his way to delight deeper into her being, not only in her body but within her soul. Time passes without us realizing that the experiences are going with it, and as it happens to one, it happens to everyone too.

At work, Philip did not have so many matters that distracted him from the uncertainty regarding the events he presented could happen for his task to come true because somehow, he had seen it in some dream and he had sometimes visualized while distracting by imagining things in the wind, but he had no idea what the events would be like that fate would choose to take him to that moment.

That day he thought of going to visit The Old Lady with the White Hair but did not have the necessary time, since there was a meeting by Uicho to explain some details that they should start working on after they returned from their mealtime. Maybe, the indecisions of the raging sea of thought played its role on Philip because he decided to stay and share with everyone else as they always did at that time. Each shared a piece of whatever they got in their mules, and even food was left over sometimes.

Philip asked Chendo if he wanted to accompany them to visit his cave in the afternoon, but Chendo reminded him that they would have visits from the Jehovah's Witnesses brothers every Wednesday afternoon and that it was not possible for Mama Chayo to let him miss his reading sessions.

That afternoon, Philip took them to his hidden cave, supposedly by the place where they had gone to the lost paradise. Philip could not locate the entrance, or some vestige that showed that it was by that place, well he could not see any similar vegetation anywhere as they approached the hills, which he found very strange.

Being in the dump, looking at the horizon at sunset, the third hill on the right was where the cave was, where Philip loved to go for a long time, the same in which he spent his honeymoon with Elida. Three immense palms marked the path to the sidewalk that would take them to the entrance of the cave.

They entered a place where Philip had not been before, and they stopped behind him, in front of a rock that resembled a door, but was completely solid.

"The medallion, Philip," Gabriel told him.

Philip turned to see him touching the medallion with his right hand over his clothes, a little bewildered without knowing what it was about. He took it out of his neck and held it in his hands without knowing what to do with it, looking at them a little scared to realize that a white light glowed over their heads.

"You must use the key when you try to open it," Raziel told him.

"The key, the key. The code is the key," Philip thought, trying to visualize what his heart felt about that moment, in which he should open his true intentions.

"The bolt is presented by showing the medallion in front of the door," Gabriel told him.

He took the medallion with his right hand, while with his left he touched his heart, approached it to the stone and the stone became translucent, revealing what was on the other side of it.

"No man for many eras could achieve such a thing, Philip. You have been entrusted with a very difficult task," Gabriel told him, while he was looking at Philip somewhat insecure to walk through the door. "Wait here."

Then Gabriel and Raziel entered the door.

Philip was a little shaky by the nerves that he had to be experiencing everything that was going on vividly before his eyes, that he did not know whether to run out or get in with them too.

After a couple of minutes of waiting, Raziel came out bringing with him a gold pectoral that gave to Philip, along with the necessary instructions regarding the purpose that such pectoral had, which it would serve him to face at the time the inconveniences that present to him in the way. Raziel told him that they had the diligence to do, but that they would support him at the time he required it. That he should back to his hut and not let anyone know that he possessed the pectoral, for any reason; otherwise, everyone's life would be in danger.

"You must be worthy of the book Philip, only then you would fulfill your purpose," Raziel told him.

Philip was very confused by the words Raziel was saying to him, that he did not know what to think or what to say to him; so, at that moment he feared he would not be worthy.

"You have the key," Raziel told him. Then, Raziel entered the door, and this became solid stone again.

He hid the pectoral along with the medallion among his rags, so no one could see them. Arriving at his hut still frightened by what he had witnessed, he did not even realize how he had arrived so quickly. Elida looked at him a little scared because he stood still when he entered the hut, that not even the wood board bothered to close. She immediately asked him:

"And now, who minds disturbing you? My Quixote."

Philip took off his shirt letting Elida see the pectoral and the medallion. She approached him walking around him, admiring such a precious relic, that no man could imagine it to exist, much less could they possess no matter how much they seek in their eagerness to dominate the world.

"I don't know," Philip told her.

"I hope whatever they want from you, and that thing, do not prevent you from making love to me because I would have to appeal to Zeus himself. Well see that your new obligations as a superman do not take away those of this world; so, go wash your hands because I made you a fish and rice that my grandmother made, that would help you get back from that dumb face."

Elida was touching her belly with one hand and the other hand at the waist while claiming Philip. Having served him the dish with the food, she turned around and went to bed without saying more.

Philip removed the pectoral and the medallion and kept these in one of his trunks. He ate the last vestige of grain of rice that Elida had served him, which only left the skeleton shattered of the fish on the plate.

She was jealous someway because she felt that Philip's new heavenly diligence would one day require him to abandon everything for which he lived in this world to face his mission, which she sensed because she visualized him crying for having left behind what he loved. And that he could not return by will, not even for his bones and aching flesh to rot near his home.

After some clarification regarding the doubts, she had about Philip's fate and his spirit entrusts, Philip agreed to the request she had suggested by making love to her, with the passion with which he loved her, with the care that is taken during pregnancy, but with the same mutual delivery of disinhibitions between them.

The days pass without us realizing that we have wasted moments with misunderstandings between our interests, for the aspirations to which we cling in life. Misunderstanding ourselves first is why we fail when we try to impose reason in the face of the view that others perceive of what happens around us. Because, ignoring what the being can understand, we dare to point out the flaws in others, without understanding ourselves.

The rest of the days he was absent from everything and everyone, trying to figure out what he was living, that he did not even worry about visiting the Old Lady or talking to anyone about what was going on.

It was until Saturday afternoon that Philip asked Chendo if it was possible for them to be taken back to visit Father Joaquin. So Chendo agreed most happily because his wife had already made it up to him that they would visit Father Joaquin again that Sunday. The lady had promised him that she would make chilaquiles and cheese as a reward for taking them, that Chendo got up very early by enlisting the mule's hardware to stick it to the wagon, then he put the bags on it and a few other things for the road.

Philip was not afraid of what might happen to him, it was Elida and her baby who worried him more than anything else. He would not let anyone hurt them in any way, being willing to do whatever it takes. Feeling the love he had for them, and at the same time, what his fate prepared for him with the hints that had been given to him, he became angry and refused the fate he felt was coming upon him because he felt that he would lose everything he loved at the end of having found the reason for his personal lesson.

He could not in any way ignore the charge on his shoulders, by carrying with him the pectoral along with the medallion, placed under his clothes. Well, in his last dream he had received a warning that put him alert to wear them that day, for reasons he was yet to discover.

The morning breeze and the sunrise distracted him a little from among that sea that drowned him with worries that were not his concern, and that made him litigate against those who decide the plan of the spirit.

The sunrise made him get a little lost in the details that most ignore of their surroundings, the wind that gently caressed his face or the sunlight that gave color to things; also, the innocence with which children dealt with the issues that many men try to ignore.

As he contemplated all this, Philip asked himself, "Who am I?"

Looking to heaven, with the conviction that he asked someone else, despite disagreeing with some of God's designs for men who had perished in the past eras.

Suddenly, he recalled some words the Old Lady had told him about his fate, and how it would be presented on the paths he should choose to find his answers. Philip did not yet quite understand what the Old Lady was trying to convey to him about what might happen. He felt that he still had a lot to live, and that excited him in a very special way because he would have many opportunities to learn as much as possible to find the answers to his disagreements with the divine. Philip was willing to face whatever came bravely, despite having the fear of losing the ones he love.

"How beautiful the morning looks. Right, godfather?" Chendo asked Philip, admiring such creation.

Philip felt melancholy rising with the sun's warm, as they go on the road to the village but kept the emotion to himself for being private pains, that that beautiful dawn illuminated in his memories.

The children shut up the fuss for an instant, well they all turned to see the sunrise at that moment. Contemplating such a wonderful view, the second of the three children said:

"Santa does not exist.""I knew it before you," said the older one.

Suddenly, the innocent voice of the youngest was heard say, "Liars, he does exist," the kid said, making a fuss between them such that you did not know which side to take because you could not take away the innocent child the magical Christmas in which he believed.

Thus, we do not dare to tell them the truth either.

"How do you see, godfather? You must be ready when it is your turn to explain to your children all the lies, we tell them to be happy," Chendo told him.

"Sometimes I don't even know what a lie is or what is reality," Philip said, as he turned to see the sunrise.

The barking of the dogs brought him back to his diligence in this world, almost upon entering the village. The dogs showed no signs that their barking was of aggression, rather it was that they were happy to see them, or they expected them to throw something to eat, but they looked most cheerful around the wagon.

As they entered the village, they realized that there were people leaving their homes and walking towards the parish, also with the two elders who were at every corner bowing at the time they passed. They did not take much into account when they saw people swirl at the door of the chapel, causing Elida anguish and uncertainty in others. The children became a little frightened and hugged their father they were asking him what was going on.

Elida tried to stand up quickly while the wagon was still in motion, but Philip took her hand at that moment and hugged her against his chest, feeling what his intuition in thought had warned him on one occasion when he thought about the fatalities of what might happen.

He understood at the time, that what awaited Elida would be no good; yet he told her to calm down because perhaps it was something that had happened to someone in the village.

Elida felt Philip's intention to make her not distressed by what she had already presented in her heart, and she considered his intention, but her fears were affirmed as they approached the door where people tried to enter. They got close enough to listen to the news spreading among the people of the village, about the misfortune that had passed to Father Joaquin.

"Father Joaquin died! Father Joaquin died!" cried a lady among the people, who was crying like a sad girl, as she had lost her own father.

Some friends of the lady got close to her as Elida approached the lady, feeling her own pain when she get to know that a piece of her soul was losing a sense of life. Philip and the children immediately let go of the weeping. Even though they did not know him so well, they felt the sincere pain of those people. Well, they as the creator had tried, joined with those people in their pain. Mama Chayo and Chendo had stayed to remove the mule from the wagon, but as soon as they finished, they joined the pain of the others at the entrance of the chapel.

Chapter 8
The Book and the Prelude of Destiny

As they could, they reached the sacristy because the chapel was full everywhere of people praying and weeping for their misfortune. There were people even in the parish garden who came from all over the village upon learning what had happened to Father Joaquin.

Inside the sacristy, they found Mrs. Petra heartbroken in tears, along with two friars who tried to comfort her, while the sacristan spoke to the priest who had brought them the news.

Her heart was dissolving itself with the tears of the pain she felt, especially when she saw Elida arrive, to who she wanted to hug but she could not walk towards her of the impression it caused her the knowledge that the love of her life had died. The pain in her heart almost killed her too, by the way, she loved him. They sat her in the chair where Father Joaquin spent his reading hours, according to what Mrs. Petra told Philip when she found him in the sacristy last time. Mrs. Petra knew that Father Joaquin was a very special and mystic being, who always searched for truth, justice, and equality.

Elida immediately went to hug Mrs. Petra as soon as she saw her heartbroken, recognizing in her own flesh the pain she reflected.

"Who are you?" Asked the Priest.

"She's Joaquin's niece," answered Mrs. Petra.

The river that left her tears drowned her, and she could hardly utter those words. Well, it seemed that nothing would comfort her with the pain she felt at the time.

"Elida?"

The Priest approached her immediately, saying that it was a miracle from heaven to see that she was alive, well he knew what had happened through Father Joaquin. They were very good friends since they were in the seminary. The priest hugged her very excitedly when he realized that she was pregnant, trying to comfort her with the same intentions with which he did when she was a child since they visited him at times when her mother took her to serve different communities in the region.

"What happened to my uncle? Father Stan," Elida asked him, while Father Stan hugged her against his chest.

She had recognized the great affection he always showed her and found a little of what her family had been in him. Clinging even more to him, weeping without finding comfort in her pain.

Father Stan told her that it had been in crossfire in a confrontation between two drug traffickers from opposing sides, at the airport of the state city. And, two more people accompanying Father Joaquin had been killed as well.

He did not give many details of what had happened, he merely recounted what had supposedly happened according to the authorities that handled the case because they had not found a relationship of interests; at least, that is what was disseminated.

"How is it possible for the righteous to pay for sinners?" Elida wondered while Father Stan hugged her again to give her some comfort.

Philip was somewhat uncomfortable about not being close to the family so as not to feel the same pain his beloved had in her heart. He kept thinking of the place his being took for the designs that the divines had entrusted in his spirit, the place that no man had ever dreamed of achieving. Well, for a long time they searched for the relics that Philip had, the men who aspired to power trying to conquer the world, thus every being is corrupted in the flesh and its pleasures.

Father Stan began to tell Elida that her uncle had entrusted him with some things, in case something happens to him. Elida regardless of material things did not answer anything, she just nodded.

One of the friars stared at father Stan, but Father Stan reached out his hand as a sign to wait for him, asking him to calm down a little. Philip realized that, just like Mrs. Petra, they showed no intention of meddling with what was going on to see where they were taking their interest, to see what they were looking for.

The other friar, seeing that the father did not ask her what they wanted to know, asked her if she knew where her uncle kept an avocado-colored book with a cherry ribbon. Father Stan turned to see Elida without saying a word waiting for her to say something. Elida was still heartbroken by the loss of her uncle, and she did not know what to tell them. She just went to seek refuge with Mrs. Petra, snuggling up with her in the sacristy chair. Philip, seeing her immediately followed her to approach the lady too, meanwhile Father Stan told her not to worry, that he would only take what Father Joaquin had entrusted to him. But he insisted that that book had been one of the many things that Father Joaquin had asked him to claim in the event of his death. That, if she knew of the whereabouts of the book and told him where it was, he would thank her wholeheartedly.

Finding some comfort next to Ms. Petra and Philip, Elida took enough breath to answer him that she did not know what they were talking about, for which Father Stan apologized and approached them telling them that he would be on their side, that he was by Father Joaquin's side, and he would do the same with all who seek good.

Meanwhile, the two friars proceeded to search everywhere for the book. Father Stan told them it was very important that the book did not fall into the wrong hands, or their lives and those who are with them would be at risk; also, he told them they would not be able to stay long because there are always those who strive to possess the privilege that God bestows on those who deserve it because there are those who seek those who keep the truth to kill them.

Philip remembered the description of the book, which was the same one he had seen in the vision he had about the island that had not touched the destruction. Unless he felt that it was the same book.

Father Stan said goodbye to Elida by kissing her on the cheek and then gave them his blessing, while the sacristan helped them finish getting things into the truck where they came from.

One of the friars said to Philip, "You have to define your path, only you have the key."

Philip stood wondering if they were on his side because he did not know what to think about at the time.

Mrs. Petra took Elida to her uncle's room to rest her grief a little because of the pregnancy she needed a little rest too.

Being in the sacristy, Philip felt again that feeling he had had last time, getting carried away by the energy he felt in the pectoral and the medallion, which led him to where he felt was the book to which they referred.

On the floor of the sacristy, there was an estrange and almost imperceptible sign, which he recognized right away. It was there the whole time and he had not noticed that it was the same sign that he had seen tattooed on Raziel's right hand. At that moment, he remembered what his godfather Chendo was telling him about the Saint and the readings of his mysterious book.

When he put his hand on the sign, a small door opened from which ascended on a silver pedestal the book he had seen in that vision. He could not believe what his eyes were seeing, and he did not even know if he could touch it. He felt a sudden chill all over his body, that immediately felt his soul come out of his chest. He could not breathe, for he leaned in the book not to fall. By putting his hand on the bolt, the book opened, and Philip felt he floated in the air. He was a little frightened but then paid attention to what was going on, so that he did not lose any detail, in case it was that he was having a vision and then he would have to remember what had happened at that time. He was sane enough to realize that he was living in his own flesh his time, that was no vision he had before. He did not expect it in any way.

He closed his eyes thinking he had gone crazy, and he was imagining all that, then opened his eyes to realize that everything was still the same.

He stared out the window trying not to think of anything that might distract him from what his soul was doing within himself, but he could not pinpoint the idea that had made him happy by understanding the reason for all things because he got lost in the endless sea of thought. That left him sad and melancholy, that he felt a deep desire to cry, at not being able to specify that moment of fleeting happiness.

The feeling of touching the ground again made him return to the moment immediately, that he stared at the book without knowing what to do.

This soil confirms to us how earthly we are by attracting ourselves to it, by reclaiming our bones and grieving flesh. Philip denied the plan that had been planned on him, asking why they had chosen a beggar that no one would hear. He did not understand why they would want him to leave those he loves so that he would venture into a destination that presented his intuitions, which he had already seen in some visions and dreams.

All that confused him in such a way that he did not know what he really wanted to do. He willingly assumed the free will that was supposedly upon all men, but he respected the designs the divine took for the spirits. Philip was always a person with a broad character of comprehension and understanding, not only because of what he had learned from the books but because of what his spirit represented in this carnal life. That gave him a certain cunning and more flexible understanding of things.

There are spirits who do not need to return to this world, but who sacrifice themselves in the flesh to give us help in our own personal and intimate journey. Not so that we may be like them, but so that, in our own way, we may take the example that they have already reached in their spirit. Their example, which they have left throughout the existence of this civilization, in every culture that emerges from the change of fortune of time and the spiritual level. The whole truth is before your eyes and within your heart.

Philip was mired in the denial of losing those he loved and did not understand how God had decided for him to take that path, leaving them behind to fulfill the mission that had been planned long ago before his birth, which he did not understand at that time in his life yet.

He took the book and put it in his backpack, then walked to the door. Then, he felt a strange feeling that seduced him pleasantly in his intellect, by giving him an idea of unimaginable power, and he thought of using that power to carry out his idea of a perfect world for his loved ones. Annihilating those who did evil could make the world better in a way he had never imagined. Because he thought that the tyrants deserved punishment for their iniquities against the innocent who paid for their egocentrism of greed.

Now he clenched his fists and clung to the idea that he always had to do good by serving others, by forgiving those who assaulted him in some way too. Closing his eyes, denying what the divine had done about his insignificant life in this world.

"Enough! What can a single man offer in the face of such a great ego?" Philip reproached the sky.

Mrs. Petra touched him on the shoulder and asked him what was wrong with him, and why he was talking to himself. Philip, opening his eyes realized that he was standing outside the door of the sacristy, where there were some people around watching him while throwing his tantrum.

The lady gave him a bowl with a drink that made him come back to all his senses, then Mrs. Petra left with Elida back to Father Joaquin's room.

The chapel was full of people praying everywhere lamenting the greatest loss that people had ever had. You could clearly see the appreciation that those people had for Father Joaquin because there were people three blocks around the parish, who lamented the loss of such a good person that always treat them with great affection. Every strongman cried that day.

Elida stayed with Mrs. Petra during the time that Philip and his godfather helped the sacristan with the things that people brought for Father Joaquin. Mama Chayo, as always in the kitchen with her three children, spent time talking about the simpler things that we ignore out of fear. She helped other ladies who volunteered to prepare something to eat for people who swirled inside the chapel waiting for the father's body.

The same people who lived around the parish offered to accommodate people in their homes so they could rest. They offered them food and water as good Samaritans, as Father Joaquin had taught them by his example, that was why they respected him with such great affection. Moreover, he always welcomed them with his understanding, regardless of the condition in which the person came to him in search of hope for his life.

An old sad man with a humble-looking, who was putting a red rose and a white rose on the altar while Philip arranged a floral arrangement at the feet of Christ, pronounced some words in that strange language that he did not yet understand. Then, with the words he could understand, heard the old man say that that would serve Father Joaquin for his new journey in the next lesson of his spirit.

Philip always wondered why the suffering of living beings. He did not understand the intention in the lesson to grow as spirits because the pain did not fit in his arguments, thus he felt that there should be a possibility that would help them understand the reason between good and bad, to those who were wrong to inadvertently hurt their fellow man or some living being. Either because of the foolishness of ignorance by not wanting to accept mistakes or by the blindness of the ego that does not let us get away from the greed that gets into our eyes every day in our lives.

"Other people's pain hurts," Philip thought while watching that old man leave the roses on the altar.

Many suffer for the happiness of some, according to the system that we have implemented throughout this generation, that has not generated any change in terms of spiritual growth. On the contrary, it has become more material today than at any other time because men are little interested in what would really help them grow as superior beings, but not to impose force.

It is understanding and mercy that will make them change in what they might find within themselves; then, all that paradise suitable for love will arise around all who attain a certain degree of understanding for all that represents their reality.

By confusing happiness with possession of goods and riches, they misunderstand their own need as spirits. Do not expect them to understand others; for that, they must understand themselves first, to see the truth that lies within their hearts, which they are inadvertently polluted amid this beast that feeds us with its banal plots for the soul, but that we all accept non-conformity, according to the aspiration to which we dedicate our lives.

Philip continued to blame society for the envy it generated in men because of this idea we have adopted of profit and value over things.

Suddenly, he understood that trying to look for a culprit out of himself, was how wrong we were all, by blaming others for what we dare not accept in ourselves first, to better understand what is not understood with the ignorance that abounds these days regarding the truth. Each judge in your own way.

At that moment when he was lost in this immense sea of thought, he looked up at the face of the bloodied Christ.

"What do we fail with your sacrifice?" Philip thought as he looked at the wounds on that man's body nailed to the cross.

Suddenly, he felt a sense of tranquility and harmony that made him feel blissful in a great way. Then he felt an irresistible fear, which cowardice took hold of him, kneeling staring at the crown with the thorns.

Raising his hands to the sky, holding a bouquet of flowers, cried with great pain within himself: "Why have you abandoned us?!"

All the people turn to see him, interrupting their prayers when they heard him scream. The sacristan and Chendo were surprised in such a way, that they did not know what to do because when they tried to approach him, they felt a strange force emanating from him that prevented them from approaching him. In a few seconds, the force disappeared, and his godfather tried to help him to stand up, asking him what was wrong with him. But Philip did not let him help him and stood by himself and told him that he did not know what had happened to him, that he had only felt a lot wanting to cry suddenly. Chendo already knew him very well, so he did not ask him anymore or insist on helping him.

People began to be impatient to such an extent, that the murmurings became sporadic cries, claiming to see Father Joaquin's body. Just as people were starting to get more impatient, a cry was heard from those on the outskirts of the village, who came to see on the way an approaching caravan. Some cried that it was about the father's body, spreading the word immediately to the chapel.

They all moved to the side of the street to let the hearse pass, which was pulled by six white perch horses, adorned with flowers around. The body was in the glass coffin they had made for him so that people could see him. The people were surprised to see him as if he was sleeping and dreaming of something very good. Well, you could see a smile on his face. People knelt as they watched him pass through, by the force of kindness that radiated his presence, even after he died.

Elida and Mrs. Petra were at the door of the chapel waiting to receive the body of that righteous man, who had only given them unconditional love.

The lady held her elbow to the wrist of her right arm as she whispered something in her ear; then, she gave her a kiss on the cheek. Philip was behind them along with Chendo, Mama Chayo, and the children.

The sacristan wept next to Mrs. Petra, with trembling hands. When she saw him in anguish, she hugged him by kissing him on the cheek, whispered a few words in his ear and the young man calmed down smiling a little, as if thanking him for the words she had said.

Philip felt strange about everything that was going on as if all that was not part of his life. But, when seeing Elida pregnant, waiting for her uncle's body, realized that all of this symbolized much more than everyone saw. Well, just like royalty the ranks are inherited, this was one of those moments when something greater than anything that men could imagine would be inherited.

Secrets are inherited from generation to generation, without anyone noticing that such a mystery exists. Being necessary for the one who possesses such truth, to safeguard it until we are told that men can understand the inner universe of their individual existences as higher spirits.

Three elders offered to help Philip, Chendo and the sacristan lower the glass box from the hearse and take it to the altar of the chapel. Elida and Mrs. Petra led the route to the altar, where each one stood on either side of the glass box weeping their reasons. There was a bishop who walked behind them burning incense, who also was a friend of Father Joaquin. They had met since Father Joaquin's parents took him to community service every week as a child. He recognized Elida as soon as he saw her, and exclaimed that it was a miracle, but that at the same time a disgrace. But he told them that only God know the reason why all things were happening; besides, he told her that her grandmother was on her way to the village and that she would arrive in about a couple of hours. He told her that her uncle Marcelino was also on his way to meet everyone in the village, and he lamented that it would be an event full of mixed feelings for all.

Elida was afraid that her stepfather would seize the moment to look for her and try to hurt her, or one of those she loved, but then she felt sheltered by the people of the village. In such a way, she gave no more importance than to the pain in her heart for losing her uncle, who had taught her so many things that she valued as the most important thing in her way of seeing the world and the people who try to live in it.

They put the glass box at the feet of Christ, before the altar that was full, as much as of flowers and people around. Philip, Chendo, and the sacristan were stared astonished by the appearance of Father Joaquin inside the box, well he wore a contagious smile that made people feel somehow a kind of conformity.

The three elders, when they looked at Father Joaquin, put their right hand at the height of the heart and their left hand on the crown of their heads, which caught Philip's attention. The three closed their eyes and lowered the left hand to the height of their forehead, uttering strange words that were already familiar to him. No one seemed to realize what they were doing as if the peace that the father radiated with his smile bewitched them all.

Elida touched her belly with both hands, meanwhile, Mrs. Petra had her hands together as she prayed at chest height, then she lowers them a little by pointing them at the glass box, at the same time as the elders touched their chest and forehead.

Philip was a little surprised at what he was seeing because he seemed to be the only one who realized what was going on.

At that moment, he noticed a very dark lilac halo, which came off Father Joaquin's forehead, it perched on top of the box and headed to the tips of Mrs. Petra's hands. His heart sped up as he saw her hands pointing towards Elida's belly. At that moment, a very bright color-changing light came out of Elida's belly, merging with the light that was in the hands of Mrs. Petra, forming a brighter light that blinked, forming shadows of all who were there, but acting as if they did not realize it. As the lights merged, returned to Elida's belly at the time that Mrs. Petra touched her belly with both hands, while uttering a few words in that rare language that Philip was beginning to draw his attention to.

Suddenly, he had a vision of a distant place in time, which made him see faces of his life as a child, and moments of his adolescence; in addition, sometimes he looked like he was out of this world contemplating the planets that revolved around the sun with a suspicious harmony.

Suddenly, he noticed the explosion that had happened to one of the jewels that sustained the purpose of the divine. Such purpose spread around two surviving worlds in which he could see the life that flourished them. In the last of his visions, he could see the planet Jupiter get lost on the horizon which formed the remnants of this heavenly jewel, that had been destroyed for reasons that troubled him greatly.

As he opened his eyes, he realized that they formed a circle around Elida. Mrs. Petra touched Philip's left shoulder with her right hand, while with the other hand she held one of the old men's hands, that in turn, they were holding hands, until the last one touched Philip's shoulder with his left hand, closing the circle. Elida touched her belly with both hands, while Philip touched his chest with his right hand, and with his left hand touched Elida's left shoulder.

The sacristan approached Mrs. Petra and whispered something in her ear, who immediately took Elida with her because the bishop who was Father Joaquin's friend had asked to speak to them alone urgently.

The three elders said goodbye to Philip very cordially, two of them touching their chest when they say goodbye to him. The last one came up to him a little closer to tell him in the ear that he hoped he can visit them once more.

"Only you have the key," he told Philip at the end, then he left.

Philip was still bewildered by what had happened and refused to fully accept what he had experienced.

He recalled the words of The Old Lady with the White Hair, who warned him about the lies, of those who possess the power to control those who live on earth.

For millennia, these men have bent on the frantic pursuit of divine power, to make them the conqueror who wields the threads of the destiny of men. Still, at that moment, he felt oblivious to such a drama, of which he could not find the reason for his position in the middle of all that.

"What do we do, fool?" Chendo asked him, with his face disoriented not knowing what to do.

Philip, seeing how confused his great friend was, worried about what was going on with his beloved, and why the bishop had asked to speak to them urgently. At that moment again, were coming to his mind the words of The Old Lady with the White Hair, that he was predestined to help others on their way so that they can find themselves, on a covenant of conformity between what they might find within their being. To then open the heart to all the facts that result from our hands and intentions, not hurting others. As a personal lesson to avoid the pain we cause with our indifference, in the hopes that others place in us.

Thus that opening will transform the desired paradise around your being. Others, realizing it, will recognize the intention in each one, assimilating the purpose. Because, in doing so, they will realize for themselves that, that is what it takes to ensure the good of those we love, without the need for physical or emotional exploitation.

Mrs. Petra opened the door of the sacristy and realized that Mama Chayo was outside with the children, as always trying to see what was going on with Elida. As soon as Mrs. Petra saw her, she told her to come over with the children right away, while the Sacristan was heading towards Philip somewhat hasty. Philip had noticed all that, remaining alert to try not to lose any details.

"Come with me, bring your godfather with you. It's urgent," the Sacristan told him.

Philip left immediately after the Sacristan and called his godfather Chendo with his hand to follow them, who also followed them somewhat bewildered without knowing what was going on. He thought that maybe they needed him to help with something. Well, I think everyone has their own feelings.

Upon entering the sacristy, the bishop explained to Philip that they had to leave immediately because there were malicious people who would try to harm them. Philip thought that one of them was Elida's stepfather, that would probably take advantage of the situation to achieve his petty aberration.

"In the end, there will only be dust left from your bones and a great absence of what you were," Philip thought at that moment, concerning that poor wretch of kindness.

He had foreseen it on many occasions as a child, and he was a little surprised at the time to see that his visions became the facts that were happening before his eyes. The bishop understood that the book had been offered to Philip, seeing that Philip touched his bag while telling him everything that was going on. The bishop knew all that, and he continue to insist that he hurry because they would take so much risk by staying.

"You know it, Philip," The bishop told him.

Philip felt great strength with the gold pectoral and the medallion on his neck, but with his left hand, he touched his bag, finding a little sanity when he felt the book inside.

Mrs. Petra made a sign to the bishop, and he opened a desk drawer, in which he put his hand to pull a small hidden lever, which made the desk move around and a door would appear that was leading to a secret passageway, leading to a level that was under the chapel.

Mrs. Petra went down first to lead the way, then Elida with Mama Chayo carrying two of the children. Chendo carried the older boy by his side holding him by the hand, while Philip and the sacristan walked behind them.

They went down to the first level where there was a corridor leading to other doors with passages to different parts of the chapel. Mrs. Petra locked the door and went to open another door leading to a lower level, with another different key that she kept hanging around her neck. The youngest child began to cry as soon as the lady opened the second door. The two brothers comforted him by begging him to remain silent, then both hugged him and took him by the hand.

Seeing the bravery of the children, no one dared to complain about their fears, and only continued to follow the sacristan, who went down first this time so that Mrs. Petra will lock up once everyone comes down.

Philip realized that they had descended a little deeper than the first level, which he understood better when they reached a corridor that made him feel somewhat disoriented by the dimensions it had. The door through which they had entered was three times smaller than the doors that were next to the hallway, which was almost as large as those of a cathedral. The rooms were proportional to the size of the immense doors, for what he could see at the last of the doors was semi-open. Well as he approached the last door, Philip noticed that someone closing it as they approached. He could see a man in a white robe and a gold belt, but he only got to see half of him because he closed the door quickly before they arrived.

He had never seen such a big man in his life, he was greatly surprised to see that he looked at him too. That man was truly tall because the height of the bolt was above their heads. Philip could see the hand of that man who closed it, that it was three to four times larger than his own hands. He wanted to stop to find out more about what had left him very surprised, but Mrs. Petra pulled him to continue to the exit. It led to a tunnel that took them out to the outskirts of the village, where two monks waited for them with the Chendo's wagon, with some food for the road and a couple of books that were given to the children.

They immediately climbed into the wagon, and one of the monks took the reins of the mule; so Chendo made no objection, even though he never let anyone do it. Except for his eldest son when he taught him how to control it sometimes when they came out of the dump looking for firewood for the fire pit.

After a while having moved far enough away from the village, and making sure they were safe, the monk stopped the wagon and got off. He told them that they would be safe from that place, that they could continue alone because the danger had already passed, and that there was nothing to worry about.

The youngest of the children said, "After what happened to us?"

The monk just smiled and held his hand, telling him that everything would be fine, that he was his friend, and that he would help him the moment he needed.

Mama Chayo took him in her arms and immediately the other two children joined them in a kind of joy because nothing had happened to them. The monk approached them to say goodbye to the children, reminding them to read the books and not to forget that the greatest wealth was within their hearts, that that was their great treasure, which they would seek equitable integrity in the face of distraction, so as not to lose any shining jewels within that great treasure. He told Chendo that he was a good man, and immediately took Mama Chayo's hand.

"You are a great beautiful warrior, that there is nothing to fear with you," he told her.

Mama Chayo felt a lump in her throat because that is how her mother used to tell her when she was a child.

With his right hand, he touched Elida's belly, while with his left hand he touched his forehead, closed his eyes, and said a few words in that language that was already very familiar to Philip, that witnessed everything without intervening in the least. His mere presence and the kindness with which he addressed them as he spoke to them made them feel at peace, pleased, and very grateful.

Everyone was suspicious in the heart that that monk was a divine being who formed in the flesh to help them awaken a little of their earthly sleep. God himself in his action of promise, that he will never leave you alone at any time, no matter how intelligible the need for mercy or comfort is. So that, in your own way, form the destiny in which you work every day in your life. Philip, thinking about it for an instant, felt sorry because he always complained about what God had done with the men who died in the flood, and how he reneged on the plan entrusted to him. Somehow, he banished the idea of him being God himself, but he felt that the idea that he was being close to God was the right one.

The monk looked Philip in the eye and then he turned around to leave but stopped after a few steps.

Turned to see Philip again and then to the horizon, telling him, "The Saints have gained answers from the high, thanks to their faith, to their sacrifice. Seek the shadow of their advice but keep your heart."

Then, he got lost in the bushes.

The rush to return to the dump took over all of them as that mysterious monk walked away, Chendo being the one who jumped right away to take the reins of the mule and come back as fast as possible.

They had no setbacks that occupied the thought of peace and tranquility that the monk had conveyed to them, and they arrived just as the amber of sunset received them as it set on the three hills on the horizon.

Chapter 9
The Birth of Moonlight

That night, in their evening talks, they took on the subject of what had happened because they were very concerned that they would have to run away without having seen Elida's grandmother and uncle. Not finding any credible answer, they let time bring clues to what they should do to get back to the village and find out more about what had really happened, of why did they have to run away to save their lives.

That troubled Philip a little because he felt he possessed a massive force in wearing the gold pectoral along with the medallion. That he could well have faced anyone and had easily overcome it just by thinking about it, at least that was what he felt when remembering what had happened. Elida was trying to return him from his delirium, touching his bare back gently with her hand and telling him how special his way was, that he was destined to do good things.

"Haven't you noticed yet?" Elida asked him, as she lay on the bed insinuating her belly.

At work, they had begun to build in those days the foundations of the entrance that Philip had designed. Not giving him enough time to visit The Old Lady with the White Hair in his mealtimes because they had to stay to try to advance the construction as much as they could. Chendo did not ask him about what had happened to them, it seemed as if he did not remember, or because he did not want to talk about it. Philip respected his decision not to comment on anything when they talked to each other about the vicissitudes that happen in everyone's life.

On the last day of work, when it comes to climbing The Zorro, Philip's thought was lost among the few clouds that crossed the sky, thinking about what to do so his family can have a better future.

"Does your family worry you?" the Saint asked him as he approached him. "The creator is also concerned about his own and protects them from any evil that tries to corrupt them." "Do you think he cares about me? Does he know who I am?"

The Saint looked at him with great tenderness and compassion and smiled a little at Philip's passing ignorance (*Daniel 2:21–22*)

The days passed with the peculiarity of the daily routine without anyone highlighting the subject. Except for Elida and Philip in their evening talks because in those two months that took to build the entrance of the work, always took care to find an idea that would satisfy them in the restlessness of finding the truth of what had happened, by discussing it in each night for a long time.

On one of those days that were almost about to finish building the entrance with the pillars, Philip turned to The Old Lady with the White Hair, to seek some help on what he should do regarding some things that worried him. Not only of his personal life but of his mission as a spirit, which has been entrusted from the top.

No man has been able with the weight of the truth entrusted to him at the time of his realization, but the truth would take him further than any technological or philosophical folly. So respectfully consider before taking anything for granted. Consider yourselves.

As Philip approached the pyramid, noticed white smoke coming out of one of the chimneys, which seem to him something related to a decision that men intend to award to the divine.

He entered with the usual prudence to where she was sitting on the blue stone that radiated a violet hue when he sat in front of her.

"Are you afraid of death? Philip," the Old Lady with the White Hair asked him, now she approached him by giving him a bowl with a potion that she had prepared for him knowing he was coming to her.

Then she continued, "You're afraid that the message won't be valued and that your words will be in vain. Even though, you sacrifice your life to try."

She asked him to drink from the bowl, which Philip did without objection.

Having had his first sip, Philip asked her:

"Why do they want to kill us?"

She approached him and touched his chest with her right hand as she told him "In this world, there are beings who poison the minds of the weak with lies of false promises, in exchange for atrocities, for reasons that you are yet to discover."

Philip thought of the obligations that everyone has in society that do not let them see the inner truth that tries to declare day by day in its indications. Obligations limit us to certain places we cling to coming back to every day.

He was a little disgruntled by what his mind did to him, which began to tremble with anxiety.

The Old Lady with the White Hair asked him to drink from the bowl once more. Philip was surprised to realize that it was sweet as honey, and immediately felt relaxed and attentive to what she was trying to tell him, while she was sitting on the blue stone, which was beginning to irradiate a dim violet light.

"You haven't told me anything about what I asked you. Why do they want to kill us?"

Philip insisted a little worried, after he had his second sip, well he would like to have clearer answers, no signals or forebodings.

The Old Lady took the spear and walked to the altar uttering a few words in that language that Philip already recognized, but who still did not know the meaning. Suddenly, a fluctuation of energy came out of the blue stone pushing him a little by the force of the explosive wave, but nothing in the room had moved even a little, which made his heart speed up in an alarming way. She had exorbitant eyes pointing the spear at him, and it looked as if a white light came out of her ears and behind her neck.

"The truth is in your heart," the Old Lady told him.

He felt so miserable before society, that he refused what she had told him because he did not fully understand why they insisted on telling him where he would find the key, which will open the door that the spirit seeks, to understand his individual lesson by being reunited with his intimate truth.

The Old Lady, knowing what his mind played in his emotions, told him:

"They want to kill you because the truth does not suit some here. And so, they will continue until they achieve their task.""What truth are you talking about? We the poor people what could we teach the greedy fools?" Philip said, denying it a little because of the ignorance he had about his mission at the time. "No one would notice what this beggar could tell them. I couldn't change them all."The Old Lady pointed the spear toward Philip, and from the tip came out a ray of light that hits Philip right on the chest. Suddenly, he felt a feeling about the book, which referred to the key that opened the door so that only the privileged could enter. In addition, he had visions of people dying for the suggestions that the words of an individual caused in their poor minds, as they commit crimes against nature, murdering innocents for the idea of superiority with which they have been deceived. He saw the burning punishment of the unjust in their own conscience, who repented of what they had caused when they were in the material world. Philip cried for them, seeing that there was no hope for the poor in the world that ruled this evil and indifferent being. Philip denied his mission once again.

"They're not going to change," Philip told her, while even crying for the unjust.

"It's not about them, it's about what's inside you," the Old Lady warned.

He got up as he could and left with tears in his eyes back to the work, annoyed by the designs that the divine had laid on his shoulders.

All that time he did not wear the golden pectoral or the medallion when he went to work, leaving them in the trunk along with the book, kept from the greed of men and their way of corrupting the hearts of the innocents.

On one occasion he was walking through the streets, and he stopped to take some shade under a eucalyptus tree on one side of the street.

From that humble house across the eucalyptus tree, a lady got out and poured water on him, and yelled at him to move from there because he sucked because he was a filthy beggar who gave pity.

"What do I care about people if they have always been miserable to me," Philip thought.

His noble and helpful nature was twisted by the dark force that poisons us with doubts and prejudices. The only thing that kept him on reason was Elida's memory and her mother's advice, which immediately changed the foolishness by the humility with which his heart always boasted by serving others. Despite the aggressive brazenness of the lady's ignorance, he decided to continue his path thinking about how to help those who ignored the truth. Philip felt sorry for the lady. "Poor unprotected soul, how much you have been deceived," Philip thought.

He was not proud of what he had achieved when they finished building the entrance of the house, nor did he care more about the objects he kept, nor visited the Old Lady, for wanting to find the reason for his existence, without the divine having to intervene. He refused one more time.

That day they celebrated the end of their work, the design he always dreamed of. They were all watching him lay the last stone, hoping to celebrate the effort of their work. None knew that Philip was the one who had designed that entrance with the pillars; so, they celebrated just for the joy of having finished one more job, not for his design or his triumph.

By then, the three months of time had been met to deliver the work to the engineer, and being Elida a few weeks away from giving birth. That worried Philip, and he was not very happy because he would not receive any credit for his design. In addition, he would be out of work at the end because he felt that the engineer would not pay them the last month, even though the work had been saved. Philip and his forebodings, so that is how it happened.

The engineer returned on a Tuesday morning on the date he had told Uicho to receive the completed work and pay him the last month they had agreed.

Chendo warned Philip that something was going on because he was painting some details inside the main building of the work and had not realized that the engineer had arrived.

"Come fool, they're fighting," Chendo told him, as he was running towards him.

Uicho and the engineer were braided fighting with punches and scratches arguing over the entrance. The reproaches that became complex over time, were reflected in Uicho's tears by claiming how unfair he always was to him; despite being his brother. They all came to the place to try to separate them, but it took more than four to keep them far enough away so they would not be assaulted. The engineer yelled at them to leave the place immediately because if they did not, would bring the authorities to take them prisoner for not doing things the way he wanted. Nor did the explanations of the Saint serve him because he was so greatly enraged that he refused to give him the part that he had promised Uicho. He told him that he did not sue him because he felt sorry for him. That he had fifteen minutes to collect his things and get all his people out of his work. They all left, no one could claim anything.

Uicho took them out of the site to talk to them, to whom he thanked wholeheartedly for what they had helped him in all the time they worked alongside him. That he will inform them as soon as he had a job to do. He also paid them that week from his own pocket.

Everyone who came from the village left somewhat sad about the situation, even so, they thanked him for the attention and teaching he had shared with them all that time, and that they would always be willing to help him in whatever was offered to him.

As they always did at departure time, they rode The Zorro to return to the dump, this time a little earlier than usual. No one said a word all the way unless just necessary and that can be solved with a few faces.

The Saint and Uicho were talking inside the cockpit of The Zorro, while Philip and Chendo silently traveled in the back.

Philip was only a little raft in the sea of thought clutched by the tempest of worries, the ego that resists abandoning the responsibility that represents the name before society, refusing to abandon the habit we inherit.

Time ran without forgiving the astonishment that they had returned early from work. Even though Elida had her forebodings, she did not bother him by questioning him about what was wrong with him and let the afternoon take him in among the passing clouds, that

Philip was trying to train in response to his concerns about what he should do.

He did not know what to tell Elida and what he should not tell her about what was happening to him internally, for not want to worry her by being close to giving birth. Philip would like her to feel safe and pleased in whatever was necessary, and he tried not to convey his insecurity or conflict outside of himself, in the space where they shared their lives; even though, without knowing, he freed some of that frustration in his countenance or his silence, of which Elida was already used to it.

She approached him from behind while Philip was sitting on the bed with his bareback, she touched him gently and say, "Your worries are my sorrows. I love you above all else, with the same love that grows within me."

Philip looked at her in the eye recognizing the brilliance of her truth, that he felt a lump in his throat for the happiness that was happening to him at the time, then they got lost in their eyes while they made love.

The money he had earned was not enough but for a few days, buying only the most basic things. They had their orchard behind the hut that they hid from the leaders of the dump, as a greenhouse. They supplied the whole thing they could in a self-sustaining way. That is why he was not too concerned about not having a job because he took care of the orchard in those days and enlarged the hole where he had put the fish a little more, as they had reproduced in such a way that they could not fit anymore.

One Thursday afternoon, while Philip fixed some tomato plants with a couple of pieces of wood, one of the leader's cronies looked at him working in the garden, and immediately left to warn his boss of the find he had discovered. The dump's leader came up with five more of his cronies, claiming to Philip, why he had to hide that place from everyone else. That he should not be so selfish and shared a little of what he had, that that should be his pay for living in the dump under his rules; besides, he should pay the debt his parents had with his family. For that, all of that would serve to pay for what belonged to him. They did not take pity on the fact that Elida was pregnant, they gave a cucumber the pleas of the two so that they would not cut the plants. Philip told them that they can have whatever they wanted, but at least they could leave the plants.

They took all the fish and pulled every plant Philip and Elida had cared for with great affection for a long time, and they destroyed everything in just a few minutes.

They only had enough left for a couple of days because it was what they had inside the hut, which by a miracle they did not enter, well they thought that nothing would be of value to that wretched beggar.

Philip told Elida not to worry, that the plants would grow again, that this would be temporary.

He had no choice but to go out to the nearest village to look for some work or scrap to sell. The truth is that it is very difficult to find valuable things on the streets of poor villages, and much harder to find something to eat.

Wandering around the village square, with the guts that were rearing in every second, looking for some that could feed him to continue walking, to look for something that could take to his beloved and his baby who was about to be born. A somewhat sturdy-looking man walked in front of him, eating a big cake. Philip noticed he had one more in his left hand inside a bag. He stared at Philip, who kept looking at him as he devoured that delicacy, without resisting the temptation hoping that he would share something for mercy.

The man devoured the cake as he could and set out to do the same with the one that was in the bag, but his appetite had been satisfied with the first. When he saw Philip, he thought of giving it to him, but not complete because he gave it a couple of very large bites, then he half chewed and threw away what had bitten it because he had already been impaled. He looked at Philip with great contempt for the appearance of a beggar he had and threw what was left over from the cake to the ground. Philip was somewhat bewildered, then he turned to look at the square and realized that a dog was in the race to grab the cake that that man had thrown to the ground. He pounced to pick up the cake just before the dog bit it, and he almost had to snatch it from the snout. Philip took it and gave it a great bite desperately, then he growled at the dog like a wild beast fighting for its prey, that the dog ran away scared by the fury with which Philip had growled.

He took one more bite, but between chews, he took some conscience and kept it inside his backpack what he had left to take to his beloved. He stood still without thinking, for he had no strength for that. The time it took what he had swallowed in feeding his body with enough strength to be able to regain his sanity, was the one that he remained unable to move a finger, and people were starting to complain about seeing him as an awkward statue in the middle of the sidewalk.

A municipal officer approached him to see what was wrong with him. Touched Philip's shoulder with the rowlock and asked him if he was okay. Philip reacted immediately and answered yes, do not worry. The officer was struck by the kindness with which Philip had expressed himself and asked him if he could help him in anything.

They walked through the square for a while until they were formally introduced.

"Marcellin," the officer said very happily. "Please to meet you." "Philip," said pleased, "Is my pleasure."

Short story, Philip told him part of his life, at least what he thought was sane and reasonable, keeping some details to himself. Similarly, the officer told him some things about his personal life.

"What happened? What, are you hungry?" the officer asked him.

Philip agreed to his invitation kindly and was very grateful to help him by offering him something to eat, without judging him by appearances. The officer had told him that his parents had educated him that way since he was a child. And that it was a pleasure to help others, without judging the limitations they may have in their social conditions.

Philip was very pleased to have found a friend so akin to his principles, that he entrusted him with some things during the time they talked, every time Philip returned to the village to find something to eat.

In those days, he had told him what had happened on the construction site with the engineer and the foreman, what had happened with the blueprint, and how he had made a better design that would not have the risk of collapsing later.

One day when he was returning from the village, realized that the leaders had formed a meeting, in which everyone from the dump was there but Elida, Mama Chayo, Chendo, and the kids. Philip came over to see what it was about and realized that a man unknown to him was next to the leader of the dump speaking to his ear. The leader asked people things about a young woman that the man was looking for.

Immediately felt that this man was Elida's stepfather who was looking for her to kill her, so he went straight to his hut hiding among the piles of garbage so they would not see him. Philip entered straight into the hut, and Elida stared into his eyes.

"It can't be, it's him," Elida said, very scared.

Philip put on the golden pectoral along with the medallion, took the book, and put it in his bag, besides the watch his father had inherited. Among other things that they carried with them, but only what they could carry.

As he could, he told Chendo not to say anything in case they asked any of them. That it would be better if he took his family to the hills, so they would not get hurt because of him. Despite what Philip had told them, they all decided to accompany them, and immediately pulled out the mule to get on Elida and they left the dump without anyone noticing. The children, as always so sane and discreet, were hugging their mother on the road without complaining about anything.

Being close to the hills, Gabriel and Raziel waited for them standing by a sidewalk that could hardly be noticed with the naked eye. When they saw them, they were very happy, and finally, they could take their first bite of tranquility.

Gabriel took Chendo along with his family and told Raziel to talk to Philip.

Raziel reminded Philip of the responsibility in his chest and the wisdom within his humble bag, which was the wisdom of the material and spiritual universe. Raziel insisted that if he were diligent with his wisdom, he could discover the truth of all his concerns. That they would have to go on alone because the cave was prepared for them at the right time.

"The truth is in your heart," Raziel told him.

Then he asked him to leave, which Philip did by taking his beloved on the mule to the cave where they had their honeymoon in the early days of spring.

In the cave, they had everything they needed so they would stay without having to leave at all. But Philip wanted to go to the village to get help for the birth, which each time seemed to bring the moment closer.

He met his friend Officer Marcellin and told him the situation he was in, but without giving the details of the people or the places so as not to compromise the place where Elida was. Marcellin gave him an address where he could go for an honest job, but that it was a little far from that place. Philip did not like the idea of separating for a long distance from his beloved and his baby who was about to be born, so he had to think about it very well to venture out to find work in that place and leave his beloved alone in the cave while he was going to prove his destiny.

Upon returning to the cave, he found that Mama Chayo and the children were with Elida, which made him feel a little less worried about leaving her alone, thinking that he could go and get the job that officer Marcellin had recommended to him.

Chendo appeared after a while with a piece of firewood and some herbs to cook. Philip asked his godfather if he wanted to accompany him to that place to see if they could find work for both, and Chendo very gladly accepted that Philip was the one with the initiative. As he knew him as a child, he knew the problem he had for a long time not wanting to get far out of the dump, that is why he was very happy to hear him talk very mature about going looking for work and being so far from where the cave was.

Philip did not tell Elida how far away the place they would go was so that she would not worry too much, but she was very well cared for by Mama Chayo and the children; still, he always cared about what might happen to those he loved, despite that, others are with them. Specially Elida is days away from giving birth to her first baby.

That night, Philip and Chendo rescued the wagon from the dump without anyone noticing. Except for Elida's friend Inés, that went with them when she realized they were pulling the wagon behind Chendo's corral. Elida and Mama Chayo knew that her husband abused her, and they were very happy when they saw her arriving with them at the cave.

Very early the next morning, they went to look for that place that Officer Marcellin had recommended. Mama Chayo gave them something to eat, and she put some of what was left in the mules they were wearing.

After six hours of walking by step of a mule, they reached a large colonial-style mansion, which was next to a river, with huge gardens full of all kinds of flowers and legumes everywhere. Philip managed to see in the distance a vineyard that stretched beyond the horizon, while they were entering through an immense arch that was at the entrance, with a large iron door, which was always open. After they had crossed about two hundred meters to reach the mansion, they got off the wagon. His godfather Chendo stood by tying the mule as he made his way to knock on the door.

After three attempts, a lady came out in a floral dress, very engaged in discussion with someone else who was inside the mansion. She paid any attention to Philip because she kept talking to that person after a while opening the door. The lady spoke with a very cheerful tone that almost screamed when she spoke.

The lady turned to see Philip and immediately hugged him by giving him a couple of kisses on each cheek. Philip's filth was left on the lady's cheeks, but she did not care at all because she did not even notice.

"Creature of the Lord, come in," she told Philip when she saw him, and to Chendo when seeing him approaching, "Come on man, come on in too."

Thinking they were there to ask for some help or something to eat.

Already inside the mansion, she sent for the lady who cooked to give them something to eat and some water for the journey. Then send for Raul, his long-term driver and butler. Raul arrived discussing with her the subject they had before Philip and Chendo arrived, of which they spoke when the lady had opened the door to Philip.

The lady's accent and her way of expressing herself made Philip feel very comfortable, for he adored her from the moment she had opened the door because there was something familiar about her that had made him think of his beloved. Philip did not say a single word, he was just looking at the lady talking about it with her butler as if they were great friends. With such confidence, to such an extent that he admired when the butler called her crazy and the lady reacted with a great laugh.

"Tell me Quixote, Is this your Sancho Panza?" Raul asked Philip when he see him astonished looking at the lady.

At that time, the lady and the butler let go of the laughter in a very candid manner, but without any malice on the part of him or the lady.

"Leave them alone, you rascal. And let us see if you go to bring them something to dress too, well it is good for these poor souls of the Lord."

Philip looked at her with great attention, for he became very familiar with her manner of speaking and her great joy, that he did not know what to tell her at the time. He only stared into her eyes with great amazement at seeing the light of love that was in her.

"Tell me something noble men. Or what, have you swallowed your tongues too?" the lady told them.

Philip told her that Officer Marcellin had recommended that place to look for a job. The Lady admired herself to hear the name of that man friend of Philip, for she immediately embraced him again and told him that he could stay at that time. She yelled at the butler to take them to a room where they could sleep, and that they could immediately start working. With some regret, Philip interrupted her by telling her the reasons why they would not be able to stay that day, but that if she wanted, they could return later because he had his wife pregnant; in addition, Chendo and Mama Chayo's sons who were in the cave with Elida. In short, he explained the problems they went through without telling her the details or names of some people, thinking that they would not be relevant, he only limited to some events to protect the place where the cave was.

The lady, hearing that he had a wife and that she was also pregnant, was greatly exalted, and she could not believe that they were in a cave hidden with the children. The lady took him by the shoulders and demanded that he tell her where that cave was because at that time they would go to bring their wives and children, that does not fear anything because she would help them wholeheartedly. She immediately asked Raul to have ready the old truck to go rescue those poor people.

Philip felt safe and protected by the light in the lady's eyes, which reminded him of his mother when she comforted him by hurting himself with something. That is why he allowed the lady to help them, showing the butler where the cave was.

They came to the place right at sunset, which illuminated the road to where Philip told them to stop because they would have to walk a little to get to where their relatives were. So, Raul immediately got off to help the lady get out of the truck. Joking and laughing all the time as if they were great friends.

The lamps Raul had brought with him to enlighten himself in the darkness had not been necessary because there were plants next to the sidewalk leading to the cave that had a kind of luminosity in their leaves, in addition to other more that were illuminated as they got closer and closer to the cave. Philip thought that would have to be the work of the Gods, feeling like something extraordinary would happen. He felt within himself that Elida needed him and hastened his step a little more.

Arriving at where the cave was, Philip was surprised to see Gabriel and Raziel outside with the children, hugged by each other.

"What's the matter?" asked Philip immediately when he saw them.

"Humility in your souls has brought hope for many worlds, Philip. The time has come," Gabriel told him, receiving him with open arms, "Come on, go."

Philip approached him and embraced him, then looked towards the entrance of the cave.

Philip entered the moment they put her on Elida's chest, even with the umbilical cord joining them. At that moment, Philip cut the cord with some effort, because the nerves he had could not cut it off, because of the impression it had caused him. Mama Chayo had to help him a little so he would not hurt the girl by cutting it. The girl did not cry when he cut off her cord, she just writhed receiving her spirit and faculties, to face the challenges that life would show her when she receives what she needs to grow.

Being on Elida's chest, Philip realized at the time their skins were touching, that he could almost see how the color of Elida's skin was transmitted into the girl's skin. At that moment, he looked at the first sip of air she took in this world, hearing later a warning cry for care, which the highest decided thus, to draw our attention to that fragile being that requires care and affection. Beautiful is the simplicity with which the creator decides what many ignore at a certain time.

"Blessed Jesus, she's a girl!" the lady exclaimed, hearing the weeping of that creature who had come into this world.

She entered the cave along with everyone else and fell to her knees when she saw the girl on Elida's chest. She recognized her immediately because it reminded her of the moment when Elida's mother had been born, well she was her grandmother.

She cried the tears of joy that grandmothers tend to release when they see their blood born, and she faded a bit from the impression. Gabriel and Raziel had to help her get close to Elida, who had already recognized her, but she could not speak because of the situation she was in, besides the knot in her throat by knowing that she was there at that very special moment.

"Emma, in memory of Grandma," said the lady.

"Emma!" they all exclaimed at the same time.

Celebrating the birth expected by the divine, Elida and Philip accepted with great joy the name of their daughter.

Gabriel and Raziel helped them get in the truck to go with Elida's grandmother back to the mansion, so they would be safer from any danger for now. Gabriel laid a stone just like the one that The Old Lady with the White Hair sat in front of the altar, among the clothes with which they sheltered Emma so that the journey would not affect her because she was newborn.

The truck they were traveling in had real eagle wings painted on each side and inscriptions that said things that motivated solidarity among men. A destination prepared in an individual lesson, which impacts the lives of everyone on the planet, at the time that the divine decided to fulfill the plan that humanity needs to free itself from their naivety about their truth.

They returned to Grandma's mansion as quickly as possible so that no one could try to hurt the new being who they were committed to caring for her purpose. Everyone in the mansion became very happy to learn that Elida was alive when they saw her arrive next to Grandma. They received her with much affection weeping with joy, even more so seeing that she had her newborn daughter with her.

The days passed with the joy of the new being who brought hope in everyone's hearts into Grandma's mansion because they remembered Elida's mother when she had given birth to her, and they took care of her as a newborn.

Felipe took care of the garden along with his godfather Chendo, Mama Chayo, who helped the cook, while the children were taken to school by the driver, besides Chendo who always accompanied him.

One day, after a few weeks of arriving with Grandma, Officer Marcellin arrived at the mansion; he was the son of Elida's grandmother. He was her uncle who had not reached her that day that they had to flee Father Joaquin's funeral. Neither Grandma nor he had learned that she had been there that day, no one told them anything so as not to jeopardize the lives of Elida and others.

Father Joaquin had been buried in the garden of the parish of the village that he loved and helped throughout his life. He was dismissed as a Saint, with the honor that deserved his sacrifice and eagerness to serve others, in the most selfless way any man could have. For he was a kind and understandable man, who was always available to everyone at the time some advice was required of him. A friend to always trust.

Officer Marcellin told her mother that something very important had happened in the contest of her foundation. Because the lady has a competition of architecture every two years in honor of her husband already deceased, with a prize for the winner of a great fortune. The resources that were obtained from the foundation she invested in helping different communities around the world, promoting respect and good education within the family. Helping low-income families and building new schools so that new generations have enough education, so that they cannot be fooled with things to do about their beliefs and ideas. He told her that he had been researching for a while on the construction that won the award for best architectural design and that he had discovered certain irregularities with respect to the engineer who had designed that construction. The engineer had committed several frauds by awarding the design of several buildings for many years. Those were designs made by other people, but he had stolen them to take advantage of the good work that these people had done with their talent, which he was incapable of doing.

He explained to her what had happened in the construction that had won the foundation's architectural prize, and that he had already taken charge of putting that charlatan in prison for all the frauds he had committed. Also brought her the money that the foundation had already paid to that phony since he had not been the designer of that beautiful architectural entrance that had won the contest. The scoundrel had returned the money on the orders of a judge who sentenced him to thirty-three years in prison for fraud and corruption.

Mrs. Jesusa Nájera, could not believe what her son was telling her and was very dismayed by what had happened, confused and not knowing what to do, therefore the prize had to be given to the winning designer of the contest, and it had been given to a con man.

Grandma asked him to take a break from that matter, as she had something very important to show him. She told him that he would be very happy to know what it was about. She took him to a window facing the garden, where Elida sat with her daughter Emma in her arms, while Philip arranged some flower bushes, aided by his godfather Chendo.

"This is a miracle!" Marcellin exclaimed hugging his mother, who wept with joy to see Elida safe with her daughter Emma in her arms, mulling her mother who cared for her in the same place where she was sitting among the roses in the garden.

Marcellin looked at Philip who was cutting some flowers for them, recognizing him immediately. Then he understood that his humble friend referred to Elida when spoke of his wife in his talks in the village square that was near the dump. But he never imagined that it was about her until that moment seeing them in the garden of the mansion.

"Mother, you have before your eyes the winner of the architectural contest of dad: Philip Adame Alvares," Marcellin told his mother, as he was pointing to where Philip was with Elida, admired for the tenderness and innocence of their beloved daughter Emma, the great offspring of their unconditional love.